ETHICS, INSTITUTIONS, AND THE RIGHT TO PHILOSOPHY

Culture and Politics Series

General Editor: Henry A. Giroux, Pennsylvania State University

Forthcoming

ETHICS, INSTITUTIONS, AND THE RIGHT TO PHILOSOPHY

Jacques Derrida

Translated, edited, and with commentary
by Peter Pericles Trifonas

ROWMAN & LITTLEFIELD PUBLISHERS, INC.
Lanham • Boulder • New York • Oxford

ROWMAN & LITTLEFIELD PUBLISHERS, INC.

Published in the United States of America
by Rowman & Littlefield Publishers, Inc.
An Imprint of the Rowman & Littlefield Publishing Group
4720 Boston Way, Lanham, Maryland 20706
www.rowmanlittlefield.com

12 Hid's Copse Road, Cumnor Hill, Oxford OX2 9JJ, England

Chapter 1, "The Right to Philosophy from the Cosmopolitical Point of View,"
was originally published as "Du droit à la philosphie d'un point de vue
cosmopolitique," © 1997, UNESCO. Translated by permission.

This translation of "The Right to Philosophy" has taken into account Thomas
Dutoit's translation of Derrida's text in *Surfaces* (http://www.pum.umontreal.ca/
revues/surfaces/vol4), which has been consulted, with the consent of the editors
of *Surfaces*, for the purposes of rendering a translation that is both faithful to the
original in content and authoritative in terms of the structure and style of the
discourse. To that extent, this translation is indebted to Thomas Dutoit's
translation as an intertextual point of citation, reference, clarification, and
revision that has assisted in the creation of this version of Derrida's text.

British Library Cataloguing in Publication Information Available

Library of Congress Cataloging-in-Publication Data

Derrida, Jacques.
    [Des humanitâes et de la discipline philosophique. English]
    Ethics, institutions, and the right to philosophy / Jacques Derrida ;
translated, edited, and with commentary by Peter Pericles Trifonas.
        p. cm.—(Culture and politics series)
    Includes bibliographical references and index.
    ISBN 0-7425-0902-8 (alk. paper)—ISBN 0-7425-0903-6 (pbk. : alk.
paper)
    1. Deconstruction. 2. Ethics, Modern. I. Title. II. Series.
B2430.D483 H8613   2002
194—dc21   2002002427

Printed in the United States of America

∞ ™ The paper used in this publication meets the minimum requirements of
American National Standard for Information Sciences—Permanence of Paper for
Printed Library Materials, ANSI/NISO Z39.48-1992.

To those who are no longer with us
yet whose love eternally lives on in the memories
embodied by our hearts, deeds, and minds:

Eleftherios, Aphrodite, Markos, Petros, Pericles,
Ekaterini, Georgios, Georgia

CONTENTS

PROLOGUE

J acques Derrida is not an "ethical" philosopher. Which is to say, he does not expound a theory of ethics with respect to articulating a "philosophy of action" or a way of *being-in-the-world*. And yet, Derrida has always been concerned with ethics as the responsibility we bear to recognize the difference of the other. Deconstruction weighs in heavily here. A good example of Jacques Derrida's deconstructive ethical stance is the lecture he first presented at the first International Conference for Humanistic Discourses hosted by the United Nations Educational, Scientific, and Cultural Organization (UNESCO) in Paris during the month of May 1991. *The Right to Philosophy from the Cosmopolitical Point of View* is the text of this meditation. The ethical ramifications of who should ask the question of the right to philosophy and where, in what space and place, is the subject Derrida addresses. The text exemplifies the moment of a deconstructive reading that is ethical and yet defies closure while working on two fronts to subvert binary logic. The analysis focuses upon how UNESCO represents a post-Kantian institution that both imbibes philosophy and is the practice of philosophy—and how UNESCO extends this intermingling of thought and action toward generating a vision of what the community of nations, states, and peoples is and should be beyond a separation between particular interests and universal aims or goals. Its combining of constation with performativity gives rise to the possibility of re-visioning the global condition from a cosmopolitical point of view as an institution that is at the crossroads of a past historicity and a future history. Immanuel Kant had predicted the possibility of UNESCO's founding, but this is only of secondary importance given the magnitude of its mission to safeguard democracy and access to public education, and therefore also, the right to philosophy. In this sense, *The Right to Philosophy from the Cosmopolitical Point of View* reveals how deconstruction can help an institution to reconfigure itself for the better by causing those who are part of it, are it, to question the grounding of the concepts they hold most dear as the keys to the perfectibility of human being. *The Right to Philosophy from the Cosmopolitical Point of View* forms the first part of this book. Let us call it the *Ur-text*.

The second section of this book is a roundtable discussion between Derrida and other philosophers associated with deconstruction, such as J. Hillis Miller, Ernst Behler, and Bill Readings. The text of Derrida's lecture ends with a consideration of some specific headings of principle and practice, of ethics and politics, that Derrida suggests could move us beyond the opposition of Eurocentrism and anti-Eurocentrism and the binary basis for an exclusionary thinking that threatens the right to philosophy from the cosmopolitical point of view. This is the point of departure for the discussion.

The last third of the book looks into the future of philosophy, through the historicity of its past. It takes up the questions that arose in the roundtable discussion regarding what has become of philosophy and the right to knowledge—the right of knowledge and its pedagogical rites—after the hermeneutical violence of deconstruction upon the archive of Western epistemology resulting in "the death of metaphysics." It presents a wider reading of Jacques Derrida's writing on the subject that seeks to resist and alter the contention that philosophy is dead by implicating it with the ethical question of the right to philosophy. Is there any good reason why we should protect and conserve the past and present of metaphysics while building upon the horizons of its excesses and limitations in order to look forward to a future for thinking? The section deals with the question of what philosophy is and how it includes the other within the historicity of its corpus to betray the image of itself as Western ideology. The attempt here is to break down the misinformed generalizations and stereotypes of deconstruction, for example, that it leads the call for a recognition of the end of metaphysics, when it does exactly the opposite by acting upon the desire to bring its history into the future. This, of course, involves an ethics of practice—a teaching and a learning that does not recognize the end of philosophy but does acknowledge its *closure* as metaphysics. The problems of community, democracy, and representation are addressed with respect to the reconfiguring and rechanneling of the violence against the archive of the West beyond the act of false mourning and a mocking remembrance of a simple, teleological death without the persistence of memory in the spatiotemporal hereafter.

THE RIGHT TO PHILOSOPHY FROM THE COSMOPOLITICAL POINT OF VIEW (THE EXAMPLE OF AN INTERNATIONAL INSTITUTION)

Jacques Derrida
Translated by Peter Pericles Trifonas

The problematic that constitutes the charter of our international meeting compels us to take into consideration, at least by way of example, two types of relation:

1. The interinstitutional relation among universities or research institutes on the one hand, and among international institutions of culture (governmental or nongovernmental) on the other;
2. The particular interdisciplinary relation between philosophy, the arts, the sciences, and the "humanities." "Philosophy" names here both a discipline that belongs to the "humanities" and the discipline that claims to think, elaborate, and criticize the axiomatic of the "humanities," particularly the problem of the humanism or the presumed universalism of the "humanities."[1]

The question of these two relations will be the background of the modest and preliminary reflections that I would like to propose to you today.[2]

1

OF PHILOSOPHY: DEBT AND DUTY

I will begin with the question "where?"

Not directly with the question "where are we?" or "where have we come to?" but "where does the question of the right to philosophy take place?"—which can be immediately translated by (*ce qui se traduit aussitôt*) "where ought it take place?"

Where does it find today its most appropriate place?

The very form of this question concerning a question (*au sujet d'une question*)—namely "where?, in what place, can a question take place?"—supposes that between the question and the place, between the question of the question and the question of the place, there be a sort of implicit contract, a supposed affinity, as if a question should always be first authorized by a place, legitimated in advance by a determined space that makes it both rightful and meaningful (*à la fois droit et sens*), thus rendering it possible and by the same token necessary, both legitimate and inevitable.[3]

According to the French idiom—and already the usage of this idiom, the effective authority of this idiom, brings us back (*nous rappelle*) to the question of the cosmopolitical,[4] and would by itself enjoin us to ask this question—one would say that there are places *where there are grounds* for asking this question. That is to say, that here this question is legitimately and rightfully not only possible and authorized but also necessary, indeed prescribed. In such places, such a question—for example, that of the right to philosophy from the cosmopolitical point of view—can and should take place.

For example, UNESCO would thus, perhaps fundamentally, be the privileged place—I say this not out of convention and not at all out of politeness to our hosts—indeed, the only place possible for truly developing the question that brings us together today. In its very form, the authority of this question in a way bears the mark (*le sceau*) of this institution, receiving from it in principle both its response and its responsibility. To say it in a word, it is as if UNESCO, and by privilege the philosophy department within it, were, if I may say so, the particular *emanation* of something like *philosophy*, of something like "a right to philosophy from the cosmopolitical point of view," an emanation that is particular for being circular, as if a source—and the emanation is always from a source—were going back to the source (*remontait à la source*). UNESCO is perhaps born from the positing (*la position*) of a right to philosophy from the cosmopolitical point of view.[5] It is properly up to UNESCO to answer for this right by responding to this question. UNESCO bears both the response and the responsibility for this question.

Why? Why is UNESCO, in its proper destination, in the mission which it has assigned to itself, the institution that today is qualified par excellence to ask this question, to do it justice in its turn, to elaborate it, and to draw the practical teachings from such an elaboration?

My subtitle transparently alludes to the famous title of a great short text by Kant, *Idee zu einer allgemeinen Geschichte in weltbürgerlicher Absicht* (1784), *Idea (in View) of a Universal History from a Cosmopolitical Point of View*. As we know, this brief and difficult text belongs to that ensemble of Kant's writings that can be described as *announcing*, that is to say, predicting, prefiguring, and prescribing a certain number of international institutions that only came into existence (*qui n'ont vu le jour*) in this century, for the most part after the Second World War. These institutions are already *philosophemes*, as is the idea of international law or rights that they attempt to put into operation. They are philosophical acts and archives, philosophical productions and products, not only because the concepts that legitimate them have an assignable *philosophical history* and therefore a philosophical history that is inscribed in UNESCO's charter or constitution; but because, by the same token and for that very reason, such institutions imply the sharing of a culture and a philosophical language. From that moment on, they are committed to make possible, first and foremost by means of education, the access to this language and culture. All the States that adhere to the charters of these international institutions commit themselves, in principle, *philosophically*, to recognize and put into operation in an effective way something like philosophy and a certain philosophy of rights and law, the rights of man, universal history, etc. The signature of these charters is a philosophical act that makes a commitment to philosophy in a way that is philosophical. From that moment on, whether they say so or not, know it or not, or conduct themselves accordingly or not, these States and these peoples, by reason of their joining (*par leur adhésion*) these charters or participating in these institutions, contract a philosophical commitment—therefore, at the very least, a commitment to provide the philosophical culture or education that is required for understanding and putting into operation these commitments made to the international institutions, which are, I repeat, philosophical in essence. (Let us note in passing that this may be interpreted by some as an infinite opening, and by others as a limit to universality itself—if one considers, for example, that a certain concept of philosophy and even of philosophical cosmopolitism, indeed of international rights and law, is too European. But this is a problem that will undoubtedly come up again in the course of discussion.)⁶

What are the concrete stakes of this situation today? Why should the large questions of philosophical teaching and research, and the imperative of the right to philosophy, be developed more than ever in their international dimension? Why are the responsibilities to be assumed no longer simply national, less national today than ever, and even less tomorrow than ever, in the twenty-first century? What do "national," "international," "cosmopolitical," and "universal" signify here, for and with regard to philosophy, philosophical research, philosophical education or training, and indeed for a philosophical question or practice that would not be essentially linked to research or education?

A philosopher is always someone for whom philosophy is not *given*, someone who in essence must question the self about the essence and destination of philosophy. And who reinvents it. It is necessary to recall this fact even if it seems trivial or too obvious. For such a situation and such a duty are more particular than it seems and this can lead to redoubtable practical consequences. The existence of places such as UNESCO, that is, of international institutions that not only imply a philosophy—indeed, imply philosophy in the discourse, and I would even say in the language, of their charter—but have also deemed (*jugé*) it necessary to endow themselves (*de se doter*) with a specialized department of philosophy. (Which is not at all self-evident and which recalls the whole debate, open ever since Kant's *The Conflict of Faculties*: Why would an essentially philosophical institution need a department of philosophy?⁷ Contrary to Kant,

Schelling thought that, since the university is nothing but a large philosophical institution, philosophical in all its parts, and since philosophy is supposed to be everywhere in the university, there was thus no reason to confine it to one department). The existence, then, of a properly philosophical space and place like UNESCO, and the fact that UNESCO's mode of being is one that is *a priori* philosophical, constitute, it seems to me, a sort of axiomatic, a system of values, norms and regulating principles in virtue of which we are here, of course, but which also prescribe every philosopher to question him or herself concretely about such a situation, and not to take it as an established and obvious fact without grave consequences.

Before drawing some preliminary consequences—less abstract than these first axioms—allow me to recall Kant's text. If it announces and prescribes a "universal cosmopolitical state" (state, *Zustand,* in the sense of the state of things, of the situation, of the real constitution, and not of the State with a capital S), if Kant specifies at least the hope (*Hoffnung*) for it, the hope that after many revolutions and transformations this cosmopolitism "in the end" (*endlich*) becomes a fact, and if Kant founds this hope (which remains a hope) on the purpose that is "the highest in nature" (*was die Natur zur höchsten Absicht hat*), this hope is everything but the expression of a confident optimism and, above all, of an abstract universalism. By briefly underlining some *limits* that give to the Kantian discourse its very form—its form at once the most positive, the most modern, the most richly instructive, but also the most problematic—and by insisting rather on the *difficulties*, I would like to introduce the presentations and the discussion that will follow—introduce them and not, obviously, anticipate them, precede them, and even less foresee them or program them.

What are these difficulties? What do they prefigure concerning the tasks and problems of our time? But also, what do they not prefigure? And what in our time could, indeed, should, exceed (*déborder*) a discourse such as Kant's?

The idea (in the Kantian sense) that brings us here together in the awareness that the definition of a philosophical task and of a right to philosophy should be formulated (*doit être posée*) in its cosmopolitical, and therefore international or interstate dimension (and it is

already a serious question to know whether the cosmopolitical traces
a link among the cities, the *poleis* of the world, as nations, as peoples,
or as States), this Idea supposes, and Kant says so himself, a philosophical approach to universal history that is inseparable from a sort
of plan of nature that aims at the total, perfect political unification
of the human species (*die vollkommene bürgerliche Vereinigung in der
Menschengattung*). Whoever would have doubts about such a unification and above all about a plan of nature, would have no reason to
subscribe even to the fact of sharing a philosophical problematic, of
a supposedly universal or universalizable problematic of philosophy.
For anybody having doubts about this plan of nature, the whole project of writing a universal—and therefore philosophical—history, and
thus as well the project of creating institutions governed by an international—and therefore philosophical—law, would be nothing but a
novel.

"Novel" is Kant's term. He is so aware of the risk that, several
times, he deems it necessary to address (*de s'expliquer*) this hypothesis or this accusation, and, for that matter, to reaffirm that this philosophical idea, regardless of how extravagant it may appear to be, is
neither a fiction nor a novel-like story. Philosophy, in the formative
body (*le corps en formation*) of its institution, is above all not literature, and more generally not a fiction, in any case not a fiction of the
imaginary.[8] Yet the danger of literature, of the becoming-literature of
philosophy, is so pressing, and so present to Kant, that he names and
rejects it several times. Yet in order to do so, it is necessary for him
both to invoke the guiding thread of a pattern of nature (the guiding
thread: that is, a convenient instrument of representation [*Darstellung*], which is not the surest way of being free from the novel) and
to also take the history of the European nations as the surest guiding
thread for following this guiding thread, first of all in its Greek, and
then Roman, beginnings, in opposition to that of the so-called barbaric nations. This is why this text, which is cosmopolitical in spirit,
according to a law that could be verified well beyond Kant, is the
most strongly Eurocentered text that can be, not only in its philosophical axiomatic but also in its retrospective reference to Greco-
Roman history and in its prospective reference to the future hegem-

ony of Europe, which, Kant says, is the continent that "will probably legislate some day for all the others."

Since this difficult and acute question of the European, indeed continental, model of philosophy for our problematic today will not fail, I suppose (and in truth I hope), to reemerge in the debate that will follow, I would like to evoke a few lines of Kant's text. They indicate that the only means of opposing philosophical reason to the novel or to extravagant fiction is, at least in Kant's eyes, to trust the European history of reason and first of all the Greco-Roman history of history. In the Seventh Proposition, Kant recalls that nature will have naturally and paradoxically used the natural unsociability of men (and Kant is a pessimist insofar as he believes in this natural unsociability of men and in the natural or originary state of war among men) to push them into contracting artificial and institutional links, and into entering a Society of Nations:

> Nature has thus again used the unsociability (*Ungeselligkeit, Unvertragsamkeit*) of men, and even the unsociability among the large societies and political bodies which human beings (*créatures*) construct and are given to, as a means of forging a state of calm and security from their inevitable antagonism. Thus, the excessive and unremitting military preparations for war, and the resultant misery which every state must eventually feel within itself, even in the midst of peace, are the means by which nature drives nations to make initially imperfect attempts: but only, after many devastations, upheavals and even complete inner exhaustion of their powers, to take the step which reason could have suggested to them even without so many sad experiences—that of abandoning a lawless state of savagery and entering a Society of Nations of peoples in which every state, even the smallest, could expect to derive its security and rights not from its own power or its own legal judgment, but solely from this great Society of Nations [of peoples: *Völkerbunde*] (*foedus amphyctionum*), from a united power and the law-governed decisions of a united will. However novel-like [more precisely, however exalted, enthusiastic, *schwärmerisch*] this idea may appear, and it has been ridiculed as such when put forward by the Abbé St. Pierre and Rousseau (perhaps because they believed that its realisation was imminent), it is nonetheless the inevitable outcome of the misery in which men involve

one another. For this distress must force the states to adopt exactly
the same resolution, etc. . . .[9]

The logic of this teleology is that we ought to be grateful to nature—and Kant literally says so—for having created us so naturally,
so originarily unsociable and so scarcely philosophical in order to
push us through culture, art and artifice (*Kunst*), and reason, to make
the seeds of nature blossom.[10]

That which resembles a novel-like story yet isn't one, that which
in truth is but the very historicity of history, is this ruse of nature.
Nature makes use of the detour of violence and of primitive, thus natural, unsociability in order to aid reason and thereby put philosophy
into operation through (*à travers*) the society of nations. Here we
would find a paradoxical incitement to today's debates in this teleological ruse of nature. Greco-Roman Europe, philosophy and Occi-
dental history, and I would even dare saying continental history, are
the driving force, capital, and exemplary—as if nature, in its rational
ruse, had assigned Europe this special mission: not only that of
founding history as such, and first of all as science, not only that of
founding philosophy as such, and first of all as science, but also the
mission of founding a rational philosophical (non-novel-like) history
and that of "legislating some day" for all other continents.[11]

In the Ninth Proposition, Kant admits for the second time that
the philosophical attempt to treat universal history according to a
hidden design of nature and with a view towards the total political
unification of humanity resembles a Novel (and here he names the
novel by its name, *Roman*). Yet in order to contradict this novel-like
hypothesis and to think human history, beyond the novel, as a system
and not as an aggregate without a plan and program, without providence, he refers to what he calls the guiding thread (*Leitfaden*) of
Greek history (*griechische Geschichte*)—"the only one," he says, "in
which all other earlier or contemporary histories are preserved and
passed on, or at least authenticated."

In other words, Greek historicity and historiographicity would
be the sign, the index, and therefore the guiding thread that allows
us to think that a history bringing together everything that concerns
the universality of humankind is at all possible. Of this Greek history

(history both in the sense of *Geschichte* and *Historie*, history in the sense of event and of narrative, of the authenticated account, of historical science), one can trace the influence, Kant says, upon the formation and decline of the political body of the Roman people insofar as it first "swallowed" the Greek *polis*, and then sketched the *cosmopolis*[12] by influencing or colonizing the barbarians, who in turn destroyed Rome. "Finally," Kant proceeds,

> we add the political history of other peoples episodically (*episodich*), insofar as knowledge of them has gradually come down to us through these enlightened nations. We shall discover a regular process of improvement in the political constitutions of our continent (*in unserem Weltteile*) (which will probably legislate some day for all other continents [*der wahrscheinlicher Weise allen anderen dereinst Gesetze geben wird*]).

The teleological axis of this discourse has become the tradition of European modernity. One encounters it again and again, intact and invariable throughout variations as serious as those that distinguish Hegel, Husserl, Heidegger, and Valéry. One also encounters it in its practical form, sometimes through denial, in a number of politico-institutional discourses, whether on the European or world scale. This Eurocentric discourse forces us to ask ourselves—I'll say this very schematically so as not to keep the floor for too long—whether today our reflection concerning the unlimited extension and the reaffirmation of a right to philosophy should not both *take into account and de-limit* the assignation of philosophy to its Greco-European origin or memory. At stake is neither contenting oneself with reaffirming a certain history, a certain memory of origins or of Western history of philosophy (Mediterranean or Central European, Greco-Roman-Arab or Germanic), nor contenting oneself with being opposed to, or opposing denial to, this memory and these languages, but rather trying to displace the fundamental schema of this problematic by going beyond the old, tiresome, worn-out, and wearisome opposition between Eurocentrism and anti-Eurocentrism.

One of the conditions for getting there—and one won't get there all of a sudden in one try, it will be the effect of a long and slow historical labor that is under way—is the active becoming-aware of the fact that philosophy is no longer determined by a program, an originary language or tongue whose memory it would suffice to recover so as to discover its destination. Philosophy is no more assigned to its origin or by its origin, than it is simply, spontaneously, or abstractly cosmopolitical or universal. That which we have lived and what we are more and more aiming for are modes of appropriation and transformation of the philosophical in non-European languages and cultures. Such modes of appropriation and transformation amount neither to the classical mode of appropriation—that consists in making one's own what belongs to the other (here, in interiorizing the Western memory of philosophy and in assimilating it in one's own language)—nor to the invention of new modes of thought, which, as alien to all appropriation, would no longer have any relation to what one believes one recognizes under the name of philosophy.

What is happening today, and what I believe has been happening for a long time, are philosophical formations that cannot be locked into this fundamentally cultural, colonial, or neocolonial dialectic of appropriation and alienation. There are other ways for philosophy than those of appropriation as expropriation (to lose one's memory by assimilating the memory of the other, the one being opposed to the other, as if an *ex-appropriation* were not possible, indeed the only possible chance).

Not only are there other ways for philosophy, but philosophy, if there is any such thing, is the other way.

And it has always been the other way: philosophy has never been the unfolding responsible for a unique, originary assignation linked to a unique language or to the place of a sole people. Philosophy does not have one sole memory. Under its Greek name and in its European memory, it has always been bastard, hybrid, grafted, multilinear, and polyglot. We must adjust our practice of the history of philosophy, our practice of history and of philosophy, to this reality, which was also a chance and which more than ever remains a chance. What I am saying here of philosophy can just as well be said, and for the same reasons, of law and rights, and of democracy.

In philosophy as elsewhere, Eurocentrism *and* anti-Eurocentrism are symptoms of a colonial and missionary culture. A concept of the cosmopolitical still determined by such opposition would not only still concretely limit the development of the right to philosophy but also would not even account for what happens in philosophy. In order to think in the direction of what happens and could still happen under the name of philosophy (and the name is both very serious and unimportant, depending on what is done with it), we must think about what the concrete conditions for respecting and extending the right of philosophy may be.

I will juxtapose very quickly here the headings of problems that are in truth systematically or structurally coordinated.

First Heading

Whoever thinks that s/he has to make the right to philosophy from a cosmopolitical point of view be respected, accorded, and extended should take into account what is—but also what has always been—the competition among several philosophical models, styles, and traditions that are linked to national or linguistic histories, even if they can never be reduced to effects of a nation or a language. To take the most canonical example, which is far from being the only one and which itself includes numerous sub-varieties, the opposition between the so-called continental tradition of philosophy and the so-called analytic or Anglo-Saxon philosophy is not reducible to national limits or linguistic givens. This is not only an immense problem and an enigma for European or Anglo-American philosophers who have been trained in these traditions. A certain history, notably but not only a colonial history, constituted these two models as hegemonic references in the entire world. The right to philosophy requires not only an appropriation of these two competing models and of almost every model by all men and women (*par tous et par toutes*) (and when I say all, it is not so as to be formally prudent regarding grammatical categories—I'll come back to this in a moment), the right of all men and women (*de tous et de toutes*) to philosophy also requires the reflection, the displacement, and the deconstruction of these hegemonies, the access to places and to philosophical events that are exhausted neither in these two dominant traditions nor in these languages. These stakes are already intra-European.

Second Heading

Respecting and extending the right of all men and women (*de tous et de toutes*) to philosophy also supposes, and I'm saying it too quickly again, the appropriation but also the surpassing of languages that, according to the schema I was putting into question just a while ago, are called foundational or originary for philosophy, that is, the Greek, Latin, German, or Arabic languages. Philosophy should be practiced, according to paths that are not simply anamnesic, in languages that are without filiational relation with these roots. If the most often hegemonic extension of this or that language, in an almost all-powerful way—and I mean the extension of English—can serve as a vehicle for the universal penetration of the philosophical and of philosophical communication, philosophy demands, by the same token and for that very reason, that we liberate ourselves from the phenomena of dogmatism and authority that language can produce. It is not a matter of removing philosophy from language and from what ties it forever to the idiomatic. It is not a matter of promoting an abstractly universal philosophical thought that does not inhere in the body of the idiom, but *on the contrary* of putting it into operation each time in an original way and in a nonfinite multiplicity of idioms, producing philosophical events that are neither particularistic and untranslatable nor transparently abstract and univocal in the element of an abstract universality. With a sole language, it is always a philosophy, an axiomatic of philosophical discourse and communication, that imposes itself without any possible discussion. I would say something analogous, or in any case stemming from the same logic, for science and technology. It goes without saying that the development of sciences and technologies (whether theoretical physics, astrophysics or genetics, computers or medicine, be they in the service of economy or even of military strategy, or not) breaks open the path (*frayage*), for better or worse, for a cosmopolitical communication, and as such opens the ways, through scientific research yet also through epistemology or the history of the sciences, for what in philosophy will have been, and always has been, in solidarity with the movement of science, in different modes. The hypothesis or the wish that I would be tempted to submit to the discussion is that, while taking into account or taking charge of this progress of the sciences in the spirit of a new era of Enlightenment for the coming new millennium (and in this respect I remain Kantian), a politics of the right to philosophy for all men and women (*de tous et de toutes*) might be not only a politics of science and of technology but also a politics of *thought* that would yield neither to positivism nor to scientism nor to epistemology, and that would discover again, on the scale of new stakes, in its relation to science but also to religions, and also to law and to ethics, an experience that would be at once provocation or reciprocal respect but also *irreducible autonomy*. In this respect, the problems are always traditional and always new, whether they concern ecology, bioethics, artificial insemination, organ transplantation, international law, etc. They thus touch upon the concept of the proper, of property, of the relation to self and to the other within the values of subject and object, of subjectivity, of identity, of the person—that is, all the fundamental concepts of the charters that govern international relations and institutions, such as the international law that is, in principle, supposed to regulate them.

Considering what links science to technology, to economy, to politico-economic or politico-military interests, the autonomy of philosophy with respect to science is as essential for the practice of a right to philosophy as the autonomy with respect to religions is essential for whoever wants philosophy not to be off limits for anyone, man or woman (*ne soit interdit à aucun et à aucune*). I am alluding here to what, in every cultural, linguistic, national, and religious area, can limit the right to philosophy for social, political, or religious reasons, for belonging to a class, age, or gender—or all of that at once.

I'll take the risk here of affirming that, beyond what would link philosophy to its Greco-European memory, or to European languages, even beyond what would link it to an already constituted Western model of what one calls, in Greek, democracy, it seems to me impossible to dissociate the motif of *the right to philosophy-from-the-cosmopolitical-point-of-view* from the motif of a *democracy to come*—without linking the concept of democracy to its past givens and even less to the facts classified under this name, all of which hold within themselves the trace of the hegemonies that I mentioned more or less directly. I do not believe that the right to philosophy (which an international institution [like UNESCO] is duty-bound to uphold and to extend in its effectiveness) is dissociable from a movement of effective democratization.

You can easily imagine that what I am saying here is everything but an abstract wish and conventional concession to some democratic consensus. The stakes have never been as serious in today's world, and they are new stakes, calling for a new philosophical reflection upon what democracy and, I insist, the *democracy to come*, may mean and be. Not wanting to be too lengthy in this introduction, I'll wait until the discussion to say more on this subject.

Third Heading

Although philosophy does not amount to its institutional or pedagogical moments, it is obvious that all the differences in tradition, style, language, and philosophical nationality are translated or incarnated in institutional or pedagogical models, and sometimes even produced by these structures (primary and secondary school, university, research institutions). They are the various places for the debates, competitions, war, or communication of which we will speak in a few moments; but, in order to conclude on this subject, I would like for the last time to turn to Kant, so as to situate what today may constitute the limit or the crisis most shared by all the societies that, be they Western or not, might wish to put into operation a right to philosophy. Beyond political or religious motivations, beyond the motivations—at times apparently philosophical—that may lead to limiting the right to philosophy, and indeed even to prohibiting philosophy (for a particular social class, for women, for adolescents not yet of a certain age, etc., for specialists of this or that discipline or for members of this or that group), and even beyond all the discriminatory motivations in this regard, philosophy is everywhere suffering, in Europe and elsewhere, both in its teaching and in its research, from a limit that, even though it does not always take the explicit form of prohibition or censure, nonetheless amounts to that, for the simple reason that the means for supporting teaching and research in philosophy are limited. This limitation is motivated—I am not saying justified—in liberal-capitalist as well as in socialist or social-democratic societies, not to mention in authoritarian or totalitarian regimes, by budgetary balances that give priority to research and training for research that is, often correctly, labeled useful, profitable, and urgent, to so-called end-oriented sciences, and to techno-economic, indeed scientifico-military, imperatives. For me, it is not a matter of indiscriminately contesting all of these imperatives. But the more these imperatives impose themselves—and sometimes for the best reasons in the world, and sometimes with a view to developments without which the development of philosophy itself would no longer have any chance in the world—the more also the right to philosophy becomes increasingly urgent, irreducible, as does the call to philosophy in order precisely to think and discern, evaluate and criticize, philosophies. For they, too, are philosophies, that, in the name of a techno-economico-military positivism—by looking toward a "pragmatism" or a "realism"—and according to diverse modalities, tend to reduce the field and the chances of an open and unlimited philosophy, both in its teaching and in its research, as well as in the effectiveness of its international exchanges.

It is for these reasons—and I'll stop here for now—that, for whatever reservations I thought needed to be made with respect to the Kantian concept of the *cosmopolis* (both too naturalist and too teleologically European), I will still cite Kant in conclusion. I will cite what he calls exemplarily an example. His short treatise, *Idea for a Universal History from a Cosmopolitical Point of View*, is also obviously a treatise on education, and it could not be otherwise. In his Eighth Proposition, after having announced and acclaimed the Enlightenment era and the universal freedom of religion, Kant writes the following, which still remains worthy of meditation today, almost without transposition.

If I had to give a title to this passage, it would perhaps be "Of Philosophy: Debt and Duty."

> This enlightenment, and with it a certain sympathetic interest which
> the enlightened man inevitably feels for anything good which he

comprehends fully, must gradually spread upwards towards the thrones and even influence their principles of government. But while, for example, our world rulers have no more money to subsidize public educational institutions or indeed for anything which concerns the world's best interests (*das Weltbeste*) because everything has already been calculated out in advance for the next war to come, they will nonetheless find that it is to their own advantage at least not to hinder the private efforts of their citizens in this direction, however weak and slow they may be. But in the end, war itself gradually becomes not only a highly artifical undertaking, extremely uncertain in its outcome for both parties, but also a very dubious risk to take, since its aftermath is felt by the state in the shape of a constantly increasing national debt (it is a modern invention, *Schuldenlast einer neuen Erfindung*) whose repayment becomes unforeseeable [repayment is *Tilgung*, the annulling, the erasure of the debt, the destruction that Hegel distinguishes from the *Aufhebung*,[13] which erases while conserving]. It is a thorny affair. At the same time, the effects which an upheaval in any state produces upon all the others are so perceptible (where all are so closely linked in our continent by trade) that these other states are forced by their own insecurity to offer themselves as arbiters, albeit without legal authority, so that they indirectly prepare the way for a great political body of the future, for which the past world has no example to show. [This incidence not only relaunches the large question of debt in terms of its geopolitical effects, which are decisive today for the future of the world, it also opens the way for a reading of Kant that is less, let us say, traditionalist and perhaps less teleologistic than what I have sketched.] Although this political body exists for the present only in the roughest of outlines, it nonetheless seems as if a feeling is beginning to stir in all its members, each of which has an interest in maintaining the whole (*Erhaltung des Ganzen*). And this encourages the hope that after many revolutions, with all their transforming effects, the highest design of nature, *a universal cosmopolitical state, will at last be realised* as the matrix within which all the original capacities of the human race may develop.

With this citation I wanted to suggest that the right to philosophy may require from now on a distinction among several registers of debt, between a finite debt and an infinite debt, between debt and duty, between a certain erasure and a certain reaffirmation of debt—and sometimes a certain erasure in the name of reaffirmation.

NOTES

1. Jacques Derrida has engaged the institutional dimensions of philosophy as a discipline and its teaching apparatus in his work on the deconstruction of metaphysics. A definitive compendium of this work is Derrida's *Du droit à la philosophie* (Paris: Galilée, 1990). See also Peter Pericles Trifonas, *The Ethics of Writing: Derrida, Deconstruction, and Pedagogy* (Lanham, Md.: Rowman & Littlefield, 2000).

2. Remarks presented in introduction to a conference organized by M. Sinaceur under the auspices of UNESCO, May 23, 1991.

3. The question of where the question of the right to philosophy should be asked, and by whom, relates to the question of responsibility for its teaching and therefore its perpetuation as a tradition and a specific way of thinking and understanding. See Jacques Derrida, "Where a Teaching Body Begins and How It Ends," trans. Denise Égea-Kuehne, in *Revolutionary Pedagogies: Cultural Politics, Instituting Education, and the Discourse of Theory*, ed. Peter Pericles Trifonas (New York: Routledge Falmer, 2000).

4. The "cosmopolitical" will be defined more specifically within the body of Derrida's lecture, but a preliminary foray into its dimensions would characterize it as those social and cultural conditions that effect the constitution of a subject and subjectivity as a hybrid global and political entity. It is not only a question of cosmopolitanism—or the wider exposure of the subject to difference—but also a question of the politicization of difference that leads to a recognition of the values of difference and their influences within the constitution of selfhood.

5. The question of the origins of philosophy has preoccupied Derrida since *Of Grammatology*, trans. Gayatri Chakravorty Spivak (Baltimore: Johns Hopkins University Press, 1974). Indeed, Derrida disarms the power origins have in Western culture by placing an ethical questioning in the way of any authenticating values that origins inculcate as a means of justifying the ideology of a perspective. Perspective always already determines the legitimation of an origin and gives it cultural currency and therefore value. Origins set forth systems of values that pave the way for cultural practices.

6. See Jacques Derrida, *The Other Heading: Reflections on Today's Europe*, trans. Pascale-Anne Brault and Michael B. Naas (Bloomington: Indiana University Press, 1990), for an extended discussion of the historical and philosophical

influences of inter-European and intra-European identity and its internal and external boundaries.

7. The question may seem tautological if we accept Derrida's argument that an institution is the manifestation of philosophy put into practice, or the practice of philosophy made concrete and formalized. And yet, it is necessary. Derrida addresses the question of the place of philosophy in the university in *Du droit à la philosophie*.

8. In "Where a Teaching Body Begins and How It Ends," Jacques Derrida details the historical genealogy of the teaching body, its conceptual and corporeal domains for the discipline of philosophy. Derrida is concerned with the construction of the teaching body as a cultural archetype and archive that determines and is determined by the scene of teaching and its institutions.

9. Emmanuel Kant, *Philosophie de l'histoire*, trans. Stéphane Piobetta (Paris: Aubier, 1947), 69–70. Along with his bracketed comments, Derrida has silently modified the translation.

10. Derrida follows the line of Kant's argument about human nature in the tradition of Jean-Jacques Rousseau, Thomas Hobbes, and Adam Smith regarding the principles of communitarianism and the ethical foundations of civil society. Like the aforementioned philosophers, Kant maintains that communities develop by necessity rather than freedom of choice.

11. The ethnocentrism of arguments like Kant's is something that Derrida originally addressed in *Of Grammatology*. The desire to interpret all cultural histories according to the archives of Western culture and its teachings propels the governing logic of colonialism and imperialism.

12. The origins of the modern-day cosmopolis can be traced globally to histories of military confrontation between localized communities such as villages or cities that engaged in forced colonization and hybridity. The pattern is not unique to the civil societies of ancient Greece (e.g., nation-states determined by the power of the *poleis*).

13. The critical moment of the dialectic, as Hegel defines it, is the moment where the opposites (thesis vs. antithesis) are synthesized into a new entity that both conserves and erases the differences between both entities. Newness enters the world via the process of synthesizing opposites through the logic of the dialectic and its reason.

ROUNDTABLE DISCUSSION

Hazard Adams
Ernst Behler
Hendrick Birus
Jacques Derrida
Wolfgang Iser
Murray Krieger
J. Hillis Miller
Ludwig Pfeiffer
Bill Readings
Ching-hsien Wang
Pauline Yu

This roundtable discussion engaged Jacques Derrida's "Of the Humanities and Philosophical Disciplines: The Right to Philosophy from the Cosmopolitical Point of View (The Example of an International Institution)," a contribution to the first International Conference for Humanistic Discourses, held in April 1994. Derrida's text for this conference was based on his lecture at the UNESCO conference in 1991, translated as the first chapter of this book.

⸽

JACQUES DERRIDA: This lecture was under another form initially when delivered at the UNESCO in Paris. As you probably know, there is the problem of philosophy being a part of this institution, and its history from the beginning of the UNESCO. So why did I choose to adapt, adjust it here? Three points, and I'll try and be brief. First, should I apologize for having left my paper in French? I should, of course. But on the other hand, I think that seeing the problem of language, and especially of the dominant and excluded languages, is already alluded to by Kant and in the paper, in different ways. I wanted to effectively—performatively, let's say—ask the question, Why read my text in French? Now, if I do so, it's not a matter of . . . antagonism or anti-Americanism, or some well-known opposition to the current linguistic, political hegemony of English, American English. It's because, on the one hand, I think that our conference, our project, bears witness to [the fact] that the Anglo-American is and will remain our medium in our discussions. Why is it so? How can we account for that? Usually, although it's a well known phenomenon that today Anglo-American is the universal language—the only universal language, effectively—the reasons why it is so are not clear, not simply a question of political or economic power. We should account for that, and have responsible answers to this current hegemony. I say this all the more in the spirit of, let's say, friendship to Anglo-American language, but I think that this hegemony is even a problem for the Anglo-American speakers. Each time I have to enter this debate (we all have to do that), I insist on the fact that the threat, if there is a threat, is not only a threat to other languages. It's also a threat to English, to some experience of English.

Second point. I thought I should put philosophy on the table because so far it's literature which has been privileged. So my questions about philosophy in this context are seven. First, as a discipline, as a discipline. Can we say that philosophy as a discipline is part of the humanities, or not? Is philosophy part of a culture, of what one calls "culture"? As you know, there is in philosophy, especially in twentieth-century philosophy, an objection to the inclusion of it in the space of culture. Heidegger, for instance, would say, "Well, philosophy is not a cultural phenomenon. When we speak of culture, we have immediately to do with multiple differences in history, in the history of the arts, and so on and so forth, whereas philosophy is like science, in that the project of philosophy is, as a project, universal. To that extent, philosophy doesn't belong to a culture." I don't share this view. There are cultural aspects of philosophy, but philosophy is not a cultural phenomenon. Then, always considering philosophy as a discipline, we all know here (all of us have been privy to this fact) that philosophy, especially German philosophy in the late nineteenth century, has played a major role in the construction of the model of the university. So in order to refer to this philosophical structure of the model of the university, in the same way, I wanted to emphasize the fact that the very concept of this international institution is philosophical through and through. That is, the concept, the charter, the constitution of the UNESCO is grounded on philosophical concepts, philosophical European concepts, and that's why it's a philosophical institution. So I think we have to interpret, to analyze the history of the academic models in Europe, in the [United] States, in the world, from a philosophical point of view. Then as to philosophy as a discipline. As we know, the place and the extension given philosophy in different cultures, and even in the West, in different nations, different systems of education, are different, but they have something in common today. This is something philosophy has in common with all the humanities: the reduction of the space, reduction of money, reduction of the power, because philosophy is supposed to be useless in our industrial societies, and it's a matter of a political struggle. In my own country, we constantly are fighting and struggling against the reduction of the philosophical space in the high schools (in France, philosophy starts in the high schools), and of course in the universities. Then my second point, philosophy not as a discipline, but philosophy as the implied or supposed authority in what we referred to yesterday or the day before yesterday as *Begriffsgeschichte*. Of course, it's not necessarily a philosophical project, but we know that implicitly the history of concepts is philosophically structured, and the authority for the history of the concepts (especially the concepts we are dealing with—culture, translation, is in principle philosophical).

A third sub-point: philosophy is supposed to be the place from which one defines (and this is not only a matter of *Begriffsgeschichte*) . . . the concepts of man, humanity, what is man, what are the transformations of the concept of man today, what is humanism—all these questions are philosophical through and through, and . . . even if we disagree with philosophical claims or philosophical interpretations about this, we have to face this philosophical claim about these concepts. And this is perhaps the most important point to me within the second point: the relationship between philosophy and natural languages, European languages. And I try in my paper to avoid the opposition between two symmetrical temptations, one being to say rapidly that of course philosophy is something universal. Today it's a well-known phenomenon—there is a Chinese philosophy, a Japanese philosophy and so on and so forth. That's a contention I would resist. I think there is [too much] specifically European, specifically Greek in philosophy to simply say that philosophy is something universal. Now saying this, I think that every kind of thinking, of thought, is philosophical. I will distinguish philosophy and *Denken*, thinking. Philosophy is a way of thinking. It's not science. It's not thinking in general. So when I say, well, philosophy has some privileged relationship with Europe, I don't say this Eurocentrically, but to take [history seriously]. That's one temptation, to say philosophy is universal. The other temptation would be the one I just sketched: "Well, philosophy has only one origin, a single pure origin that is its foundation, its institution, through a number of grounding concepts which are linked to Greek language, and we have to keep this in memory and go constantly back to Greece and back to this Greek origin—European [origin]—through anamnesis, through memory, to what philosophy is." This is a symmetrical temptation which I would like to avoid. So what I propose is another model: that is, while keeping in memory this European, Greek origin of philosophy, and the European history of philosophy, [to] take into account that there are events, philosophical events, which cannot be reduced to this single origin, and which mean that the origin itself was not simple, that the phenomenon of hybridization, of graft, or translation, was there from the beginning. So we have to analyze the different philosophical events today, in Europe and outside of Europe. This avoids at the same time Eurocentrism and simple-minded anti-Eurocentrism. That would be the last subpoint in the second point.

And the last, the very last point, would have to do with philosophy and literature. Why then choose this among other things? There are many reasons for this choice, but I won't summarize them now. I'm thinking of the reference that Kant makes to the *Roman*, and the way he tried to distinguish between philosophy and the novel. And we have here a classical philosophical gesture in the philosophical exclusion of literature—philosophy becoming what it is or what it should be by simply avoiding literature. That's why I've chosen this text. The way . . . Kant tries to avoid literature or the novel—*Roman*—is precisely [a] reference to Greek history. . . . [H]e says, "In order to contradict this Romanesque hypothesis and to think the human history, beyond the novel, as a system and not simply as an *agrégat sans plan*, a programless aggregation, or composition, then we have to follow the living thread of Greek history, the only one which transfers or translates (*transmette*) all the other histories which have been prior or contemporaneous. . . ." So it's again through reference to the Greek origin that Kant claims that indeed one can, of course, purify philosophy [of] literature. And I think this might be one of the places for discussion here.

ERNST BEHLER: Well, my task is now to respond to you, and I will do this by outlining a number of topics we might like to discuss and to which you might like to respond, but I will also refer back to your paper—not by way of summarizing it, just by picking something here and there. And what I consider most important in the first place (it would be my first point) in your paper and in your presentation is that it puts philosophy onto the agenda for a group that is usually inclined to deny the difference between philosophy and literature. Of course, what you articulate is a special type of philosophy. It is not the systematic type of philosophy as Kant develops it in his *Critiques*. It is more philosophy in the sense of his popular writings, namely, the writings on faculties, on history—that is, a type of philosophy that he himself defines as *Weltweisheit*, "world wisdom." This philosophy speculates about things that, according to the *Critiques*, are forbidden to speculate about. You cannot speculate about the end of history or the further course of history, because that's a transcendent use of reason. In these texts, Kant does it nevertheless, although the first *Critique* forbids it.

And how does he do it? (And this is perhaps a second point). I want to say that the reason literature does not show up in this text is that literature is not in his purview. He is not concerned with literature. When he talks about education (and education is an essential matter in these essays), it is philosophy that does education. You still have this idea in Hegel, in Hegel's *Encyclopedia:* edu-

cation is done by philosophy. Literature is too multifac-
eted and might confuse the mind of the student, whereas
philosophy goes straight to the subject matter. How does
philosophy proceed in the case of Kant? With an utmost
attempt at self-criticism. The end state of history, the cosmopolitan state, is not just around the corner. This is a
long, arduous process in which we are involved. Kant
uses terms like "infinite progress," progress without end,
for that. Only toward the end can we vaguely perceive
what will come. This is what Kant puts in as self-critique
of his own attempt. It's arduous. You have described this
on the basis of the model of nature. Hegel calls it *schlechte Unendlichkeit*—"bad infinity," "poor infinity"—
because it does not articulate itself, it does not come to
an end. The final state of cosmopolitanism is never there,
it's in the process of becoming and will perhaps never be
achieved. This is an important point, in my opinion,
which is also contributing to the overcoming of Eurocentrism and of finding a position beyond what you call the
antithesis of Eurocentrism, that is, an anti-Eurocentrism.
It's precisely this moment of eternal becoming, I would
say, that matters for Kant. Let me describe this a bit. Kant
would say (these are my words), "Yes, I am Eurocentric.
Yes, I am deriving from Greek history and I am national-
istic. However, I have now reached a point in history
when this appears to be over, when the moment has
come to turn cosmopolitan, and to turn away from na-
tionalism. However, this won't be achieved in one moment. This will be an infinite process, and during the
course of this process, we will always encounter new hin-
drances, new obstacles which we have to overcome."
This is how I would try to rephrase Kant's attempt at
overcoming Eurocentrism, namely, by describing a process that is infinitely going on. One last point: the "development of all originary faculties, or dispositions, of the
human mind." This state is not just to be enjoyed socially
for Kant. No, that would be Hegelian, or Marxist. This

state is also to be enjoyed on the individual level. The development of all the potentialities of the individual is of course also for the benefit of the infinite process. These are some of the themes that I would like to articulate before I open the discussion.

DERRIDA: Thank you for what you just said. First, you noticed the question that I ask at the end of my paper: no money, there is no money. What will the state sponsor, given the military investment, and so on? I think it's a question which is a current one. Now, speaking of infinity, of this infinite process, my concern is this one. First, given our project, do we inscribe it in the horizon of a new community? Do we have to build a new universal community, or should we change the axiomatics of this cosmopolitanism. And from that point of view, I would say that (without of course wanting to be untrue to the memory of the Enlightenment) I think that today we have to rethink cosmopolitanism, given the new situation. For instance, I'm sure that all the crises that the international institutions are experiencing now, we know (I think this is true) that they have—we have—to rethink the concepts . . . of state, of sovereignty, and so on, which are European concepts, and which are at the center of the constitution of these international institutions. These international institutions were foreseen by Kant. In a certain way, they are Kantian in spirit. So on the one hand, I would say that there is an infinite perfectibility. We have to improve. We shouldn't interrupt the work of these international institutions, the United Nations, the UNESCO, and so many others. It's something good and we have to improve them. This is an infinite process. But at the same time, it's not a continuous infinite process. We have to try and displace some concepts which are absolutely essential to these constitutions. It's not a matter of speculation, of speculative movement within the academy. What happens today in Bosnia, in Israel, and in so many places, compels the states and the nations to transform their own assumptions. And this is not simply a continuous progress, but sometimes a break . . . in the concept of state, in the concept of internationality, in the concept of "citizen of the world," and so on and so forth. To do this, we need philosophy. That's why the question of teaching philosophy is not simply a question for teachers and pupils. It's a worldwide political question. If the citizens of all the countries are not learned, some of them, in philosophy, they won't understand anything [of] what's happening, not only in the newspaper, but in the decisions of the state, the decisions of the [UN] Security Council, and so on and so forth. Even if we think that we have to deconstruct some tradition, at the same time we have to insist that these traditions be taught, and taught more than ever. So philosophy is everywhere, philosophy is everywhere, today more than ever. And so, in order to avoid the dogmatic use or exploitation of this philosophy, teaching the discipline—that is, strengthening the people professionally—is . . . is a duty.

Now this question of the place for philosophy, the topos for philosophy, is a very strange question. For instance, in the German debate between Kant and Hegel [and] Schelling, about Humboldt—the place of philosophy within the university. As you know, some of you are, like myself, interested in this problem of the conflict of faculties. On the one hand, you have Kant, who says, "Well, philosophy is and should be a department, a faculty—the lower one, under the theological, medical, and law school, but at the same time, the only place where we should be absolutely free to say whatever we want, provided that we simply speak directly and don't try to make performatives." You have this view of philosophy, occupying a circumscribed place, however privileged it may be. And then you have Schelling's (I think it's Schelling's) view. He said, "Well, the university is philosophical through and through. We don't need a department of philosophy; philosophy is everywhere." So is it a choice between two logics? Is it a choice? I would say no. Philosophy must be everywhere, is everywhere—not only in the university, but on the radio, within the speeches of the politicians, and so on and so forth. It is everywhere. It is everywhere in the academy. There is philosophy at work in literature, in physics, and so on and so forth. Nevertheless, in addition to that, we should have a specialized training, professional training, for philosophy. Otherwise . . . philosophy everywhere could become a terrible dogmatic weapon. So that's a paradox in the topology of the discipline.

MURRAY KRIEGER: Just very briefly: you speak more benignly than one would have anticipated of both the two kinds of philosophy, the analytic American and the continental. And certainly the problem of where philosophy is on the menu, and whether it's part of the agenda of humanistic discourses obviously rests on the relative hegemony of the analytic, Anglo-American tradition, which has held power up until now and probably for some time to come, given the nature of academic politics in the United States.

DERRIDA: The linguistic hegemony cannot be dissociated from the hegemony of a type of philosophy.

KRIEGER: Exactly. And departmental philosophy is not only exclusionary, but the single tradition which gets traced back. But also, of course, it would exclude the rest of the humanistic discourses. I mean, it's back to the original notion that philosophy is not one of the humanistic discourses, but stands apart from them as the explanatory instrument for taking care of all the other uses of language. And to that extent, of course, there's no place around this table for most philosophy as it is taught in most parts of the United States.

DERRIDA: Yes, I agree. Two points, Murray. First, I said that the hegemony of the Anglo-American is all over the world, it is irreversible, something we shouldn't even try and resist. It's done. Everyone in the world will have two languages, his own plus Anglo-American. Then without trying to prevent this, we have to handle this differently. This is not only a linguistic phenomenon, because it goes hand in hand with the fact that today no theoretical work, no literary work, no philosophical work, can receive a worldwide legitimation without crossing the [United] States, without being first legitimized in the States—we know that. That's a serious problem. It's not simply a problem of language. It is also a problem of language, but it is not simply a problem of language. And then we also know that in so many cultures, so many cultures in the world, the hegemony of the analytic philosophy is obvious. It's obvious in Asia, and it's obvious in . . . many parts of Africa.

KRIEGER: I didn't know this, by the way. You're saying something I really had no idea about. The Anglo-American analytic is everywhere?

DERRIDA: In Scandinavia, even sometimes in Germany. But among the many problems which link with this phenomenon, we have the fact that analytic philosophy has little to do with the humanities.

KRIEGER: That's my point.

DERRIDA: The affinity between philosophy and literature is between continental philosophy and literature, with a few exceptions. So the problem of the humanities, of the humanistic discourse is also this problem—that analytic philosophy, if it is a serious problem, it is because there is also, despite this hegemony, some decadence.

KRIEGER: But also more defensiveness.

DERRIDA: Yes, more defensiveness. But they don't pay any [attention] to arts or to literature (with some exceptions).

HENDRICK BIRUS: Well, it's in some respect a situation like in the sixteenth century, the domination of European thinking by the Latin language. All had to be translated, all relevant thoughts had to be formulated in Latin. And maybe there will be in the future some struggles like between the vernacular languages and the Latin language.

DERRIDA: It's unlikely to happen during our lives. You mean a new language will . . . ?

BIRUS: There will be no advantage for French or German maybe, but Chinese or . . .

DERRIDA: Spanish.

BIRUS: Yes, but my point is the following. What could be seen as an antagonism on the linguistic level [and] on the philosophical level, is much more a problem of internal relationships. For instance, that English has become a universal language, that really is a danger for English as a "natural language." It is the domination of spoken and written English by . . .

DERRIDA: . . . of a certain English.

BIRUS: Yes, . . . [a] lingua franca. And it was one step in the Latin tradition of Latin language, to restore a true Latin against the lingua franca, that Latin spoken by the scholars and others. But on the philosophical level, there are two interesting problems. On the one hand, if you try to debate the real philosophical problems of the worldwide dominating analytical philosophy (as you, Jacques, did it in *Limited Inc.*), you have to deal with the Vienna circle, with Wittgenstein, with Kant, and with the continental tradition as a whole. So you have to bridge the Channel and elaborate these technically encapsulated problems. And on the other side, there are also tendencies in Anglo-American philosophy to ask for other roots and for other areas of their own philosophy. For instance, encouraged by Heidegger, Stanley Cavell's question of the philosophical impact of Thoreau.

WOLFGANG ISER: Given the professionalism of analytic philosophy, those who leave the camp are considered defectors.

BIRUS: But there are very interesting outlaws, and I think they are more and more encouraged.

DERRIDA: I agree, I agree.

KRIEGER: Yes, the point is that Cavell precisely is excluded by the high church, but there is a high church. The important thing is this, that once we have conceded the tremendous priority in the universities of the sciences and of technology, we must recognize that what gives the authority and the power and a continuing place to analytic philosophy is the fact that it is what helped unlock the philosophy of science. Having worked hand in hand with some of the leading theorists in science, they're more interesting to the people who count because they keep doing their work. What they do with respect to us and the fact that they're not interested in sitting with us or in dealing with the kind of works that we read, is not going to bring them down because they have the key to the door that opens to the palace, and we don't.

BIRUS: But that is not a philosophical question, and I asked for philosophical questions.

KRIEGER: I know. But probably one other point about ours being the lingua franca: when you spoke of the disadvantage that is for us, the biggest disadvantage is one that we've all talked about, the fact that it creates a nation of persons who speak one language. Jacques said everybody around the world is going to speak two languages, his own and English. And the result is that here we are trying to discover cross-cultural relations, and we have an entire country without the languages to carry out any of them.

BIRUS: But that isn't true. You have Hispanics, you have Chinese—you have internal linguistic problems, I think.

KRIEGER: But hardly into the second generation. Pauline had to learn Chinese in a university, not at home.

BIRUS: In New York, advertisements are bilingual. Why?

KRIEGER: Yes, but for a first generation.

J. HILLIS MILLER: I think it's going to change a little. I think these languages will last a little longer, begin maybe to last a little longer.

KRIEGER: Maybe. It's hard to know. There are so many political pressures against it.

MILLER: Two things. One: I have an anecdote which certainly bears out what Jacques was saying about the imperialism of analytical philosophy. When I was in the People's Republic of China at the Chinese Academy of Social
Sciences, I was with a delegation to bring news to the
Chinese mainland of the new developments in many different fields—political science, business management,
literature (I was the literature person), and philosophy.
The philosophy person was John Searle. And we all had
to give little speeches in the presence of distinguished
scholars from different institutes of the Chinese Academy of Social Sciences (David Easton was the political
scientist) about our fields. And Searle told them: "I have
news for you. We have developed in England and the
United States a definitive method in philosophy which
puts an end to all previous philosophy, which is called
logic and analytical philosophy, and . . . everybody recognizes this as the predominant philosophy, and it needs to
be institutionalized very rapidly here in this large country." And he said this without any irony at all, and without any sense that there might be any other possibility
. . . That's the anecdote.

The second thing is really more on the question. It
seemed to me that in your preliminary remarks and even
in your paper, there is a loose thread that I'd like to ask
you to pick up a little more. You said in your preliminary
remarks, "I chose this text of Kant because of the word
Roman and of the explicit connection between philosophy and literature." You didn't really go on to do anything with that, and then when I listened to you talking
about[how] . . . philosophy is everywhere, we all have to
do philosophy, philosophy should be taught in the
schools, and so on, . . . I thought of the passage from
Kant. Obviously you chose it also because it's not just

literature that uses the word *roman*, with its connotations not only of the novel, but of the Roman.

DERRIDA: The Roman and the Greek.

MILLER: Roman/Greek, that's right. Well, he says in the passage you quote, "however romanesque, more precisely exalted, enthusiastic." So "romanesque" and "exalted, enthusiastic" are somehow related to one another. Remember that I said I side with Proust, and said it made me comfortable to know that Proust says, "[If] you want to learn about politics, read the *Recherche*." You now seem to be opposing philosophy and literature, and I'm interested in having you expand that relationship just a little bit. Obviously you don't want to be Kantian about this, but what is the relation for you between philosophy and literature if it's not the Kantian one? You see the point of my question. That is to say, it's a serious question.

DERRIDA: I know it, I do.

MILLER: Is there any element of the literary in the kind of philosophy you're saying we all have to learn? And if so, what? Or is it simply that our concept of literature, like so many of the other concepts you named—translation, all the rest of it, and therefore the very institution of literature, how we define it—is simply a philosophical one, so that not only the study of literature as a discipline, but even the writing of literature and the existence of it is simply philosophical through and through, and in that sense dominated by these philosophical concepts? You said you were not an imperialist for the philosophy department, but it sounded a little bit to me like that. And it did occur to me at some point in our discussion to remember that all of us around the table here are Doctors of Philosophy. We're called "Doctors of Philosophy" in memory, I take it, of that Humboldtian university that defined everybody who gets a graduate degree as a Doctor of Philosophy. I don't know anything about philosophy, but I have a Ph.D. I'm not a Doctor of Literature.

BEHLER: May I briefly interfere at this point? The systematic question remains on the table. Just a historical obser-
vation: when Kant says that he does not want to engage
in a *roman*, he is not referring to the highest type of literature. *Roman*, "novel," at that time, is no poetry at all, it's
prose, "romanesque," something popular. The systematic
question remains for you, Jacques, but on the historical
level, Kant tries to find a middle position between strict
speculation in the strong philosophical sense of the *Critiques* (and he doesn't do this in the essay) and fiction,
mere invention. This type of philosophy has a thread,
and this thread is of course very interesting.

MILLER: It would be as if you would talk today about . . .
What do you call those novels that everybody reads?
Harlequin romances . . . *romans* . . .

BILL READINGS: [There is a] difference in French between
a romance and a *roman*.

MILLER: Nevertheless, a lot is at stake, because the passage
here says that if you don't believe in the Kantian plan of
nature, in which it's natural, absolutely natural, that
there would be a development towards these international institutions—if you don't believe in that, then the
only alternative to that is the Harlequin romance, that is
to say, something that's not only literature, but literature
of a base and popular, corrupted sort. I agree with you—
that's another reason why it's important, this *roman*. . . .

BEHLER: So there are three levels of discourse at stake. One
is the hard philosophical level, which we are not discuss-
ing here. Then there is a middle level of philosophy in
the sense of world wisdom, which makes use of reason
in an unjustified way. And then, finally, you have fiction,
mere fiction.

DERRIDA: Hillis, I gave up answering such an enormous
question a while ago, but I'll try an elliptic answer, because it's impossible for me to say something short and
clear. Just the elliptic answer would be this one, perhaps:
I think that the concept of literature is a philosophical

concept. At least it's impossible to build this concept without some philosophy. Now at the same time, I would say that literature, some events in literature (I wouldn't speak of simply all literature), . . . the ones [that] have interested me most, . . . resist this philosophical concept of literature. That is, there is some invention or some events, some happenings, in what one calls "literature" which constantly undermine or displace the philosophical stabilized concept . . . of literature. So that's why I'm, as a "philosopher," interested in literature—not in *any* literature, but in this kind of literary displacement, a writing which displaces the philosophical assumptions about literature—now my, let's say, gesture here cannot be simple. I'm often accused, especially by some American philosophers, but also German philosophers, . . . of . . . reducing philosophy to literature. Habermas said it publicly without shame that for me a text by Artaud or Genet and a text by Hegel is the same thing; it's homogeneous. Of course I would never say such a thing, and I try to respect the limits in the functioning of what one calls a literary text and a philosophical text. But at some point, at some point, I think that since they share their belonging to a natural language, there are at work within philosophical—so-called philosophical—texts, texts which are legitimized by the institution, by the academy as philosophical texts—there are in these texts some structures which could be considered literary or which have something to do with literature. Well, that's what I said the other day. For me there's no essence of literature, but there is a specific functioning of it. The same sentence, sometimes the same philosophical sentence— *Cogito ergo sum*—which in a given context is obviously a philosophical statement, can become, in a different context, in a different set of statements, a literary, poetic, or anything-else statement. And this, among other things, because what philosophy shares with literature is its dependence . . . on natural language. There is no absolute formalization of philosophical language. That's why the problem of philosophy and culture, philosophy and natural language is so important. So I want to be free to respect the distinction, the rigorous distinction between philosophy and literature, and at some point to examine what in literature is philosophical. And there are a number of points where philosophy is, which can be not only interpreted as philosophemes, but which you couldn't understand without a philosophical tradition. Wordsworth—you can't read Wordsworth without knowing a lot of philosophy as such. The same with Baudelaire, with Mallarmé, of course. And on the other side, there are in philosophical discourse poetic events, and there are poetic inventions in the very act of thinking philosophically. So for me it's very complicated, so I give up really on answering such a question, at least in so brief a time.

HAZARD ADAMS: There are philosophers who have written on Wordsworth who would have been better off without their philosophy, I think.

MILLER: Knowing some philosophy doesn't guarantee that you'll be a good . . .

ADAMS: Huh uh. And that raised the question of what we call the philosophical concept of literature. It seems to me that one of the problems, at least in my knowledge of the profession of philosophy, is that that philosophical concept of literature has not changed much in response to literature's evasion of the concept. And that, in a nutshell, is one of the problems that we face in our relation to philosophy departments. Would you say that was true?

DERRIDA: Yes, I agree with you.

ADAMS: The philosophical concept of literature hasn't changed much since what Plato said in *The Republic* about the war between philosophy and literature. And I think you can see that history continue right into the analytical school of philosophy.

DERRIDA: I wouldn't say it hasn't changed at all, but the changes cannot match, of course, those in literature. Hegel's concept of poetry is not Plato's concept.

ADAMS: If that is the case, then . . . I'm not going to ask you a question it's impossible for you to respond to.

KRIEGER: But your argument in general is that the philosophers' concept of any particular phenomenon is belied by what the phenomenon might do to exceed or violate it. You complain about their trying to have a philosophical concept of translation that would apply to all the different sorts of things that go by this word. The philosopher's concept of literature, you say, cannot stand up against the differential character of what happens, for example, in China, which might not be fittingly called "literature" at all. So what is the relation of the concept to the terms?

DERRIDA: I would be inclined to generalize and say the same thing for everything, but without implying that a philosophical concept is something given by Plato and remaining in place.

KRIEGER: Yes.

DERRIDA: There is a history of the philosophical concepts . . .

KRIEGER: But there's always the struggle . . .

DERRIDA: . . . and philosophy tries to readjust itself to what's going on, to the movement of science, the movement of literature. So . . . this adjustment is historical. What happened between Plato and Hegel's *Aesthetics* is a number of literary . . . poetic [or theatrical events] . . . which forced Hegel to readjust his concepts. So you have to think of this historically.

KRIEGER: But any particular event in any particular time, you have suggested previously, can never be sustained by the concept. It must always be deconstructed.

DERRIDA: What I say in my polemics with Searle [is] that according to the concept of the concept, what is a concept . . . ?

KRIEGER: And there is something of that sort in your concern about our using the word "translation" too easily, our using the word "literature" too easily, and the trouble we will get into when we get into other cultures, which may or may not even have terms for these things, which might have conceptions so radically different as not to allow them.

DERRIDA: That's why, Murray, although I often shout [in] saying the opposite, I never speak of "the philosophy" or "the philosopher" or metaphysics as a totality. . . . There are, within philosophy and within metaphysics, breaks, mutations, heterogeneity, and so on and so forth. So I don't think that there is "the" philosophical concept of something. There is a struggle, there is a tension. Even within a relatively stabilized concept, there is a tension at work which continues to make it work and express itself. So there is no such thing as "the philosophy," even if, for the sake of convenience sometimes I say "philosophy." And if I were to be rigorous, I wouldn't even say "philosophy."

BIRUS: You would say "thinking," *Denken*.

KRIEGER: Still a problem.

DERRIDA: Still a problem. I would try to keep a gap between philosophy and thinking, [though] the gap is not the same in German and in French. In German, well, since Heidegger, we oppose *Philosophie und Denken*. *Denken* cannot be reduced to metaphysics or to philosophy. What Heidegger does with the opposition between *Denken* and *Philosophie*, or *Denken* and *danken*, . . . doesn't work in French. So if I say in French *"philosophie et pensé,"* it's something different. So I try in my own language to draw a line, an antithetical line between *philosophie* and *pensé*. But it's not the same line—although I've been inspired by Heidegger—it's not the same line as Heidegger's. Of course "philosophy and thinking" is closer to Heidegger than *"philosophie et pensé." Pensé* is another . . . semantic regime. But I try not to, let's say,

reduce any kind of thinking or questioning to philosophy, not even to reduce philosophy to questioning, the
way Heidegger, at certain points, did.

BIRUS: So you ask again the Heideggerian question of the
relationship between philosophy and philosophical
thinking as related to institutions and *Denken,* thinking,
pensé, that is beyond or at least not defined by institutions. On the other hand, the opposition between literature and philosophy means two historically changing institutions. On the basis of these institutional limits, you
can ask the questions of *écriture* in philosophy.

DERRIDA: Well, first, when Heidegger [pays] attention to
philosophy as an institution, he doesn't mean all the time
the academic institution. There is, of course, for him [a]
close relationship between some sort of philosophy, especially the systematic (in the narrow sense of "system"),
and the . . . German academy. But there is a broader sense
of institution, and in this broad sense philosophy is associated with an institution, but not necessarily with an academic institution. Now I wouldn't say, nevertheless, that
thinking as such is free from any institution [or] institutional roots. There is no, . . . on the one side, philosophy
or philosophical institutions, and on the other side, free
thinking. No. I think that thinking is always also compelled by institutional norms and forms, and displaces
them. And sometimes it's within an institution, within
the limits of an institution, that a philosophical or a
thinking event may occur, then displacing the structure
of the institution.

BIRUS: It's related to institutions, but not defined by them.

DERRIDA: Not exhausted, not exhausted by them. Yes.

KRIEGER: Could you speak a little more about one element
in the paper and that you referred to in your talk? I think
you said at one point in your remarks that you opened
with today that Western philosophy is privileged. I
thought you said that Greek or European philosophy is,
in a way, privileged.

BIRUS: Could I add to this? You say also that philosophy is *bâtarde* in this regard.

DERRIDA: Yes. And my statement is a bastard from that point of view. . . . Because I say at the same time, you cannot use the word "philosophy" and refer to philosophy while ignoring its Greek origin. Otherwise, we would simply treat the word "philosophy" as a conventional word. So it is Greek, it has been Greek, which doesn't mean that philosophy in its history is philosophy only to the extent that it refers to the Greek origin. Even at the origin, in its Greek moment, there was already some hybridization, some grafts, at work, some differential element. So I think we could, at the same time, recall the Greek origin, the link that philosophy keeps with the Greek memory, and nevertheless welcome events which have totally displaced this Greek memory . . . Egyptian, Jewish, Arabic, and others. And the difficulty we have, and Heidegger has, in assigning an origin, whether it's Plato or whoever . . . This origin, even in terms of language, in terms of poetics, the way language was treated—there is no homogeneity, there is no single origin. And that's why there are events. . . .

CHING-HSIEN WANG: This is a very interesting discussion. I was a little confused in the beginning by your conversation, between the presenter and the chair, about the theory that philosophy is the right thing to teach, whereas literature is not for education. But then in the process, you mentioned something else. I think Pauline will agree with me that for about two thousand years the Chinese educators wouldn't use stories or novels to teach students because they [thought] that kind writing would confuse the students. And that's exactly what you define in the process for us. So the Chinese educators did perceive and somehow share that idea, your explanation of Kant's idea about what to teach to the students and what not to teach. In connection with this, I do have one question here. I like to use my own language and ask, do you think philosophy is an organizer of thought, or is it a generator of thoughts?

DERRIDA: It's a terrible question because I would like not to choose between the two and others, organizing and producing, . . . generating. There are structures of, let's say, speech acts which at the same time, in the same movement, produce and organize. A performative, for instance, is something which produces an event while using, organizing a given . . . material. Words exist. We have the treasure of grammar, the treasure of a lexicon. You have conventions. All this has to be organized in form. We have to shape this. So we shape, and at the same time, we generate something new. So every . . . new event, every newness, is at the same time shaping and producing. So I think if there is such a thing as philosophy, we could demonstrate that it is a reflection on what is, a question about what is, and the question and the reflection is what we call organizing. It shapes, it comes after the fact. There is being, and we have to think and to organize our way of apprehending it. But at the same time, the new experience, the new approach, the answer to this question is an event. It's something which produces some new thinking. So I wouldn't choose between the two. If you look at the history of philosophy, every . . . great philosopher thinks or pretends, claims that he is simply reflecting, recollecting what has happened, describing . . . being. And he answers the question, What is being? Or what is history? The answer to this question doesn't, in principle, . . . generate anything. It's just a reflection, a description, a constative gesture, a theoretical gesture. But at the same time, it's a praxis which produces a new structure, a new event, a new language, and it's something we do all the time, that is—organizing and generating.

BEHLER: Jacques, a number of participants want to comment. However, since I'm moderating I want to establish a line of thought in order to keep everything nicely to-

gether. Since we have discussed your concept or your notion of philosophy so thoroughly, we want to know
whether you claim that it is not Eurocentric, that this notion of philosophy propels you beyond the antithesis Eu-
rocentric/anti-Eurocentric. Is that a correct understanding?

DERRIDA: Yes, I said two things at the same time, which
means that I'm not sure that there is such a thing as Europe, or . . . Europe as a center, or [a] center of Europe.
So in fact what I had in mind is of course about Europe,
about what we call "centrism" in that case.

KRIEGER: What could be Eurocentric without there being
a Europe, out of a self-deceiving notion that there is a
Europe and that we know what it is, even if we don't?

BEHLER: Yes, but on the other hand, if someone like Kant
or Hegel or Heidegger starts out with this notion of
Greekdom, of what the Greeks are, that is a clear Eurocentric line, whereas with the multiple use of origin and
beginning you avoid this.

READINGS: I was originally going to ask something that
you've already been asked, which is, What does philosophy name? And I want to ask you a question which is
based on noting what seems to me an interesting and
really productive irony in the relationship between the
description you've given of philosophy, where you have
both a functional and an institutional history of usage
which is hybrid and multiple, and an attempt to hold together something like the fact that it is a Greek word.
And I want to relate that to your initial point (which I
think is absolutely right), which is that the world hegemony of English is not simply a matter of technological
power; it also has to do with the way . . . the English
language works as opposed to the French language, the
historical absence of an academy or any solely prescrip-
tive institution concerning the language. And I wanted to
sort of ask you something, which is: It seems to me that
the relationship between prescription and use you've

given in your definition of philosophy could be interestingly related to the relation between prescription and use
in the development and modification of the English language, and the kind of flexibility and universalism that
the English language has in relation to, shall we say, the
French—and the reason for the English language's replacing it as lingua franca, which I take not to be solely
historical, but also to be the question of the way in which
bastardization, graft, and hybridization has proved so
much more successful in English. One other footnote. In
a sense I would say your notion of philosophy is in that
peculiar and paradoxical sense much more English or
Anglo-American than Anglo-American philosophy,
which is philosophy ceasing to be philosophy because it
is becoming expertise.

DERRIDA: Two points. I remember in my so-called debate
with Searle, I tried to show him (unsuccessfully) that he
was more of a continental philosopher than me, that
he . . . (without knowing, because I think he hasn't read
Rousseau) . . . is more Rousseauian than I am. So that's
why I share Hendrik's point that it's not a matter of antagonism. We have to cultivate the differences within
each bloc, so to speak. Another point. Perhaps what I'm
doing is more translatable finally, despite a number of
difficulties, . . . into the Anglo-American culture than it
seems. And perhaps there is something like that which
accounts for the fact that I'm so generously received in
this country, because perhaps there is something which
is not in my language, but in what I'm trying to say,
something which fits. . . .

READINGS: I have two things to say. One is that you have
to look at the very peculiar historical underpinnings
(Hillis brought in the *OED*). There's something very interesting in the way philology develops in the Anglo-
American world that is important there, and also the way
literary criticism and phenomenology is split is funny.
But I'm wondering whether this has something to do

with the question of how you could have a nonabstract universalism, in a peculiar sense. That is to say, when I say it's more English, I'm not thinking in terms of your reception in England and America so much as in terms of the question of what kind of planetary model that would imply for a kind of contagious and bastard philosophy.

DERRIDA: If I had, let's say, a philosophical political stand in that respect, I would say that I'm of course attached to a universalism which wouldn't destroy the idioms. That is, how is it possible to keep the idioms—that is, the differences in language—alive without giving [away] the Enlightenment, the universalism—without, let's say, instrumentalizing the language too much? I don't think it's possible to de-technologize the language through and through. I think that . . . even in the most poetic events, there is some *technē* at work, so it's impossible, I would think, . . . to oppose poetry to technology absolutely. Now, nevertheless, I would advocate a universalization which would be an experience of translation respecting the absolute singularity of the idioms. In that case, we would have organization and generation of new events— that is, the production of a new language, of new languages, a new experience of precisely grafting, hybridization, and production of new singularities. This implies another concept of cosmopolitanism, because the eighteenth-century concept or Kantian concept of cosmopolitanism was a concept implying a secularization of language, the sort of transparency of universal language in the abstract and technical sense. Now I think the experience we [have] now of the new nationalisms and the attention paid to the minorities' differences call for another kind of cosmopolitanism, taking into account the idioms. . . .

BIRUS: In this context, Goethe's latest use of the term *Weltliteratur* is of special interest. He wrote in a letter (April 24, 1831) about the translation of his last botanical writings by the French-Swiss Ferdinand Soret: "Some main

passages, which my friend Soret couldn't understand in
my German, I translated in my French; he translated
them in his own, and so I firmly believe, they will be
more generally intelligible than probably in German. . . .
These are the immediate consequences of the general
world literature; the nations will take hold faster of the
mutual advantages." And another example is his appreci-
ation of the efforts of Victor Cousin and his school; with
respect to them he said to Soret (October 17, 1828):
"These men are on the way to effect a reconciliation of
France and Germany by creating a language quite capable to facilitate the communication of ideas between both
nations."And such an intermediary language is not a destruction of the idioms, but a bastardization that leads to
the creation of new idioms.

KRIEGER: This is very brief, and really addresses this, but
also it recapitulates Bill's question or way of putting this.
As I understand it, you're proposing (and you represent
Jacques as proposing) that there is something—the word
"indigenous" is not the word I want, but let me use it—
within the English language that predisposes it to serve
as lingua franca. What I'm thinking of is [that] the real
flowering of bastard Englishes with many varieties begins to occur, I think, in a period after the move toward
its becoming a lingua franca is established. And I'm wondering whether we really can think of English as having
peculiar potentials.

READINGS: There's absolutely nothing inherent in it. It is
simply a historical accident concerning the peculiar relationship of England to [the] Enlightenment and to the
question of the nation-state and the way in which linguistic policy is pursued. I view this as a historical accident which produces a bastard language. I think of
America, and I think it was Jefferson (correct me if I'm
wrong) who proposed discussion of the language to be
adopted. They considered the plan that the language of

the United States of America should be Greek, and this was seriously considered.

MILLER: This was so it wouldn't be the language of the colonizer.

READINGS: Yes, but also it has something to do with an idea that English gets institutionalized in a way that allows this flexibility. I am not at any point arguing that there's an inherent *Geist* in the English language which makes English more supple and flexible. I mean, it is also a historical bastard language, in a very straightforward way, which gets invaded early on.

KRIEGER: How pure are the language systems? And given the multiple imperialisms that we have flourishing around the world for centuries, how could they be?

READINGS: As French gets reinvented, Italian is invented . . .

KRIEGER: Yes, that's my point.

READINGS: . . . and English [isn't], and that's all. I mean there may well be other languages of which I am completely unaware. I'm really arguing . . .

KRIEGER: Why is there not the multiplicity of possibilities in other nation-states that have colonial empires speaking their language?

READINGS: They have these Enlightenment academies that reinvent their language on rational principles. . . . [Y]ou have the *Academie française,* which says if you say "*le week-end,*" you're out.

KRIEGER: But that didn't keep French from being a lingua franca for centuries after they did that.

READINGS: In a very restricted way.

MILLER: I feel like an ant crawling across the enormous expanse of this question about the relation of literature and philosophy, and if you just answer three easy questions, then my mind will be at rest. But it does follow from further discussions we had where you spoke of the "performative event" quality of philosophy as opposed to its simply descriptive quality. And my questions are three very specific ones. In those moments in philosophy that are literary events (you used that word), are they essential to the philosophy, or are they excrescences that could be, you know, a kind of mistake? For a minute Descartes was literary, and if we're interested in literature we find those . . .

DERRIDA: Essential, I would say.

MILLER: Second question. . . . [T]hose literary moments in philosophy, are they any longer definable by the philosophical concept of literature . . . ? You began by saying that the notion of literature was a philosophical concept. And the answer is . . .

DERRIDA: I would say no.

MILLER: The third question, which I'm a little unclear about, is whether these events—since you're calling these literary moments "events," and therefore, since they're language, whether that leads you to say that literature as an event has something to do with a speech act, a performative use of language? The question is whether it's an accident that you speak of those literary moments in philosophy as events, and then go on later on in your discourse, in answer to the question about whether it's descriptive or constitutive, to say, "Well, it's an event, it's a speech act, it's performative." Is there a relationship between that aspect of philosophy and these moments which you call "literary," . . . which are not definable by the philosophical definition of literature, but which might be events, [that is,] constitutive, . . . and in that sense speech acts or performatives? And I'm not sure about that. I'm not trying to lead you down some kind of path.

DERRIDA: If we say "events," it's for many reasons. One is because they are singular, they occur just once. But it doesn't mean that they simply occur with no premises. For instance, the *cogito*: if you consider the *cogito ergo sum* as an event, this doesn't prevent you from knowing that before there is an enormous history, even in the history of the *cogito*, with Saint Augustine and so on and so forth. There is the history and there is the event which transforms the situation. Now if this event is, in some respects, a literary one, it doesn't happen just once at the moment when it is produced. There are many ways in which one can consider some literariness of the *cogito*. One is because it's impossible as an event without its relationship to language, to any language. Then because if you reconstitute it, then [in] the whole structure of this event you have to take into account the fabula, the fiction. So there is an intrinsic fictionality at work in this *cogito ergo sum*. Now this poeticity [was not] registered or recognized at the moment when it was produced. That's why it's only a function. It's much later, perhaps in the twentieth century, that we read things differently. It's a process. It doesn't mean that Descartes was a novelist or a poet, but this can be read today as involving some literariness, some poeticity. And this is still in the process, in the collective process, and it's not the signatory who decides whether he writes literature or he writes philosophy. That's why I insist on the functionality. Perhaps it's easier today to read Descartes as a poet than it was at the time. So it's a matter of a determined community which constantly reexamines the literariness or the philosophicity. These are not essences. There are no natural philosophemes or natural works of literature. They are functions in the same languages. The same statements, grammatically and in their lexicon, can function here as everyday language, here as philosophemes, and here as poems, as poetic sentences. It depends on the context of the interpretation—of the conventions, the agreement or disagreement—and it's always a matter of discussion. Sometimes in this ongoing discussion, in this process, there are moments of great stabilization. Everyone agrees that *The Critique of Pure Reason* is a major philosophical work, but [that] may change. Or there are some works—Rousseau, for instance, . . . in France, . . .

is not considered a philosopher. His name was not on the programs of the philosophical competitions until two decades ago. So there are canonizations, . . . legitimations, and it's a process of assigning the functions.

MILLER: A good many of our analytical-philosopher colleagues would not view Kant as a philosopher. That is to say, they would say that there's no reason any longer to read Kant. . . .

DERRIDA: And within a single corpus, there are works that you consider major at some point and minor at another.

MILLER: It's just as a colleague of mine is reported to have said to a student, "There's no point any longer studying Flaubert. As far as I'm concerned," she said, "all of the works of Flaubert could be burned. It would be no loss."

KRIEGER: It's the problem of Conrad that you were mentioning yesterday.

ISER: If I may come back for a moment to the notion of the "universal" in philosophy. It is not culture-bound, but a universal in the normative sense of the word.

DERRIDA: That was a reference to Husserl, in fact.

ISER: Yes. But is that not also the plight of philosophy? A universal is not something free-floating; basically, it has to fulfill a function. It is invoked when something has to be assessed, organized, or even generated. Thus it becomes entangled in a particular situation which may split a universal into those features that are relevant for the purpose concerned and those that remain eclipsed. Does it mean, then, that philosophy turns into a rescue operation, trying to restore the character of the universal as something in and of itself? This could well be a reason for the plight of philosophy, as it would have to adopt a stance outside or beyond the universal for it to be determined.

DERRIDA: That is, everywhere there is some universality, some philosophy is . . .

ISER: If philosophy claims to be universal, it is always engaged in certain things which philosophy is going to do.

And the moment you do any certain operations which will have repercussions on such a claim . . . Is philosophy all-encompassing? Or does philosophy become self-reflexive as it has to restore its claim of being universal, in view of the fact that it tries to solve problems which may not be universal by nature? Through disentangling itself from the tasks performed, it seems to elevate itself into its own subject matter. Should that be the case, then, universality stands in need of being redefined.

KRIEGER: That is, if there's something else, too: that its claim to a universal is like the sort of thing we're speaking about with respect to translation; it plays always against the awareness that its universality does not cover the particular application you want it to have. As Jacques was saying, the concept "literature" cannot contain the initiating events of the next literary work it comes upon, which is outside the concept—at least the one that explodes the concept. . . . Universality is always conscious of its own inadequacy.

ISER: Well, is that the case? I would be inclined to say that in each of these instances, what claims to be a universal loses its innocence. Universality may always be on the verge of losing its innocence, because it is prone to become functional.

DERRIDA: I think no philosopher would ever dispute the history of philosophy as trying to constantly correct itself, adjust itself to new contents without losing its universality.

ISER: True.

DERRIDA: The universality that Rousseau refers to is not a given universality. He was struggling against the tide at the time. He would not deny that the philosophical works, languages, systems belong to some extent. So they were radically determined. But the philosophical project as such—the pretensions, the . . . philosophical claim—is a universal one. So it's in the name of this claim that constantly philosophy has to readjust itself to for-

malization in order to integrate new contents, new determinations, and so on and so forth. That's why if we keep
Rousseau's example, at the same time Rousseau was
claiming that phenomenology, through reduction, and so
on, could reach the absolute certainty beyond any doubt
of a *cogito* again. This is absolutely universal, immediately universal, but nevertheless historical. There is a
transcendental historicity with a transcendental ideal. So
at the same time you would say, "Well, we have an absolute ground in the *cogito,* in the *ergo cogito,* and because
of this ground, which is beyond any doubt, we can build
an ideal phenomenological community with an infinite
historicity. In trying to comprehend, to embrace new
contents, new determinations, new sciences, the progress of sciences is also infinite, and philosophy should
be able to measure itself against this movement." I'm not
subscribing to this. But I'm just describing the process.

ISER: Sustaining such a claim implies [deconstructing] all
the trappings in which universality parades. If so, then,
philosophy claims toward universality, and constantly
getting functionally entangled, produces stretches of
wasteland as it is constantly in negotiation with itself.

DERRIDA: Don't think too quickly that I'm on the side of
deconstruction against philosophy. We shouldn't give up
this effort to universality and to try to think what's happening in science [and] politics, and to formalize [phi-
losophy's] own language, and so on and so forth. That's
why deconstruction is nothing against philosophy.

ISER: I did not really intend to subject what you had said
to deconstruction. Still, if you look at the current situation—especially in Germany—in which philosophy is
concerned with its own history, you get another manifestation of how philosophy is always involved in and tries
to cope with situations. And such an involvement is built
into philosophy's claim to be universal.

DERRIDA: Which implies not only an attempt to integrate
new scientific events—technology, political events, what

happens today with the international institutions—we have to build a new role for the philosophical past.

ISER: So the universality would be the changeability of that.

DERRIDA: Changeability . . . I think for me, well, Plato is an example. I think [his work is] something that we have to read again and again. It's a task . . . as urgent and necessary as the integration of a new role, new scientific results, and so on and so forth.

WANG: I just have one comment. . . . I always think poetry is universal. In your discussion about the importance of the universality of philosophy, I see that if I just [replace] that word "philosophy" with "poetry," it sounds almost the same.

DERRIDA: I have no objection, except that the way it exists, it hasn't meant poetry all the time. Although I understand that today a good philosopher could write good poetry and vice versa. But I would not like to simply drop the name philosophy, although I agree with you that there is no essential difference between some poetry today and some philosophy. But I think that each time an event—be it linguistic or not, or a written event or not—each time an event produces more universality, [the more it] . . . opens the way, it is at the same time philosophical and poetic. Each time there is a sentence which finally calls for translation, provokes translation, becomes legible and attractive and interesting for someone in another language, in another country, then there is something philosophical and poetical occurring at the same time.

ADAMS: I think, Ching-hsien, you're saying that the most particular things of poetry are the most universal.

WANG: Are you thinking about particular things like events, histories?

ADAMS: The recourse to the image, I suppose, is what I'm talking about. At the expense of turning us to the vulgar here, I'm going to ask a vulgar question. What would you do about the relation of philosophy to the institution, or the departments of philosophy to the institution?

DERRIDA: To the institution?

ADAMS: To the university.

BEHLER: He means a particular university.

DERRIDA: Some facts to start with, some facts. . . . Perhaps you know that I'm considered a professional philosopher in my own country. I teach philosophy. I'm institutionally a philosopher.

KRIEGER: We believe you.

DERRIDA: It's a professional definition in France. I'm invited and appointed here now, I've been here for seven, eight years. I've almost never met a philosopher in this university. I'm probably partially responsible for that, but only partially, I would claim. Why? Well, . . . sometimes some philosophy students come to me, and they tell me that when they name, not me, but some philosophers I'm interested in, such as Nietzsche or Hegel, the professors simply laugh at [them] and say, "Well, this is not philosophy." So you have an example here of the hegemony of the analytical. Now, another fact which is more recent (perhaps some time I would like to discuss this with you). I have some signs this year that something is slightly changed. It was almost the same at Yale—not exactly the same, because at Yale there were some philosophers with whom I could speak. Well, I would hope that some philosophy is taught in this university outside the department of philosophy, in English or in comp. lit. I'm sure I have nothing against the teaching of analytic philosophy. I would advocate some tolerance and some variety, more differences.

KRIEGER: Hazard can tell you that when he was dean, he offered a free very fancy [full-time appointment] to the department of philosophy if they would hire a continental philosopher.

DERRIDA: Changing the reference, I would say this (I have this experience in France): I am in favor of academic freedom and the autonomy of the academic field, but I know that sometimes, to change something within the corporation, the intervention of some power outside frees the situation, is necessary. Sometimes—I know that in France—the current of philosophers is simply reproducing itself constantly, constantly, and if there is no intervention from the state, . . . or from some who are outside, it will reproduce itself for centuries without accepting anything new. And I'm sure that if you don't impose on the philosopher[s] that they appoint someone totally foreign to their own school of thought, nothing will change for centuries.

KRIEGER: Do you remember at the first day or second day of our meeting this week, you spoke of the violence of censorship? You spoke of Rushdie, and so on, and I said at that time that there are other kinds of censorship that are not so violent, but just as effective without killing anybody.

DERRIDA: I know that. I've experienced this all my life in many countries.

KRIEGER: You meant when you spoke of democracy, and we said, within democracy, too, you believe in freedom within the university, but the university can legislate itself into a state of censorship.

DERRIDA: In France, for instance, there is what I call the reproduction. It is perfectly democratic, legal. There are votes, elections. Nobody's guilty of anything illegal. It's simply that they elect their disciples, and the disciples elect their own disciples, and so on and so forth, and no one comes in.

BIRUS: Like a bad Xerox copier.

READINGS: This is based on . . . [a] rather strange complaint, but an accurate one, which is that the French universities work as a medieval guild, in a way. I mean, I think there's a really interesting difference between the American university and the French university in terms of the fact that the French university has never quite had its modernity. I mean, it's never been modern in the sense that the American universities have developed. The question of reproduction for centuries: If the American philosophy department doesn't do something, it will disappear. It will disappear into local expertises. . . .

DERRIDA: Because of the market, too.

KRIEGER: Except for the technical, the scientific people.

READINGS: They will disappear away into other things.

ADAMS: There are moves in some philosophy departments to attach themselves to the sciences.

PAULINE YU: Cognitive sciences, computer [science,] . . .

ADAMS: . . . or to the social sciences. In Washington, the philosophy department reports to the Dean of Social Sciences.

KRIEGER: And in some ways, the IDP, the interdisciplinary program, that has attracted the biggest names at Irvine is the IDP in the History and Philosophy of Science, which has a very distinguished mathematical social scientist and a number of people from the physical sciences and the philosophy of science.

ADAMS: Of course this problem potentially exists in every department, but it seems to me that more is at stake for the university with respect to the situation of philosophy vis-à-vis the rest of the institution than almost any other.

DERRIDA: I described a reproductive mechanism. It is not simply a mechanism, because the reproduction in the defensiveness is increased in situations of threat. That's why, thirty years ago in France, they were more interested: because the philosophers didn't feel threatened by some other philosophers. So it is because of the structure of the philosophical field that this reproductive defensiveness . . .

KRIEGER: My son is an analytic philosopher. And an anecdote goes with that.

MILLER: If only you'd allowed him to see the film, it would have been different . . .

KRIEGER: My anecdote is that when he was doing philosophy at UCLA, I remember it was at the very time when Rorty's *Philosophy and the Mirror of Nature* came out. The bookstore kept buying dozens upon dozens of copies, and they were being bought up overnight—being bought up, of course, by all the philosophy students. UCLA then was a major philosophy department in America in the analytical mode. And apparently the tightening up of the department with respect to its attitude toward its dogmas (which my son didn't see as dogmas) . . . was, in our conversations, totally evident to me with every additional copy of the Rorty book that was sold. That is, what you said about the closing of ranks and the circling the wagons was strenuously demonstrated, because the Rorty book [marked] the first institutional awareness that something was happening, something that they couldn't control—and by one of their own, since Rorty made his early reputation as an analytic philosopher.

BEHLER: The time has come to conclude this last session and to thank our presenter, Jacques, and also the two organizers of these interesting sessions, Murray and Wolfgang. Thank you.

WHAT COMES NEXT? OR, AFTER DIFFERENCE: MEDITATIONS ON THE DEBT AND DUTY TO THE RIGHT OF PHILOSOPHY

Peter Pericles Trifonas

THE DEATHS OF PHILOSOPHY: OF METAPHYSICS AND MOURNING FOR THE ARCHIVE

That philosophy died yesterday, since Hegel or Marx, Nietzsche, or Heidegger—and philosophy should still wander toward the meaning of its death—or that it has always lived knowing itself to be dying (as is silently confessed in the shadow of the very discourse *which declared philosophia perennis*); that philosophy died *one day, within* history, or that it has always fed on its own agony, on the violent way it opens history by opposing itself to non-philosophy, which is its past and its concern, its death and wellspring; that beyond the death, or dying nature of philosophy, perhaps even because of it, thought still has a future, or even, as is said today, is still entirely to come because of what philosophy has held in store; or, more strangely still, that the future itself has a future—all of these are unanswerable questions.

—Jacques Derrida, "Violence and Metaphysics"

To mourn the death of philosophy, or metaphysics, after decon-struction resonates as premature. For the "work"—or the econ-omy of the internal emotional and psychic labor—that sustains the logic driving the motivational force of this hyperintellectualized (the-oretical) act of grieving is inopportune. Its effectivity mistakenly pre-supposes a common and universal recognition of the end of an episte-mic tradition rooted in the rise of the Occident as an archive of teaching and learning. The *force* of this mourning of philosophy mo-bilizes and is mobilized by a lamentation of the violence perpetrated against the Archeology of the Letter, its *arkhē* and *telos,* the beginning and the finale of the history of metaphysics. Regret for the "pure loss," as Jacques Derrida has called it, for an *ideal consignment of knowledge,* leaves a space (*kenosis*) for the possibility of an assem-bling or gathering (*Versammlung*), *a coming together,* of that which would mark the scene of a new beginning onto the futures of think-ing, with no programmable end in sight. What will therefore arise *from within* the irreducible anteriority of the somatico-psychic expe-rience of "philosophy" is the ineffable opening of metaphysics itself unto the threshold of an impossible unfolding.[1] And yet there is no sense, when dealing with an unforeseeable futurity *within* and *with-out* the body of the textual field of the *logos,* to philosophize "*à corps perdu,*"[2] passionately, impetuously, with desperation, Derrida would say, so as to attempt to master the outside limits of knowledge and the inexhaustive multiplicity of its sub-versive domain:

> Which does not amount to acknowledging that the margin maintains itself within *and* without. Philosophy says so too: *within* because phil-osophical discourse intends to know and to master its margin, to de-fine the line, align the page, enveloping it in its volume. *Without* be-cause the margin, *its* margin, *its* outside are empty, are outside: a negative without effect in the text *or* a negative working in the service of meaning, the margin *relevé* (*aufgehoben*) in the dialectics of the Book. Thus one will have said nothing, or in any event done nothing, in declaring "against" philosophy that its margin is within or without, within and without, simultaneously the inequality of its internal spacings and the regularity of its borders.[3]

A hyperidealized vision—that in its mad rush of looking forward to an epistemological breakthrough of infinite possibility beckons a restoration of order beyond the encyclopedia of tradition, bereft of any connections to "a past" and leaving behind or ignoring the historicity of a body of thought and thinking—can only be a "natural" (read, "uncritical") reaction. The *phthora*, a fraying, untangling, or wearing-away in degradation of the spatiotemporal organization of the struc-turality of the archive, after all, destabilizes the dimensions of the de-cisive and indivisible set of points tracing the hieratic lineage of the *meaning of metaphysics,* the *metaphysics of meaning,* and in the proc-ess minimizes the already myopic perspective and perspicacity of those hoping to actualize those first steps of faith toward the enact-ment of an impossible time—a postphilosophical era.[4]

A word of caution, however, is worthwhile here, as it distin-guishes the two horns of the dilemma of the *ouverture* of metaphysics and the fathomability of its Other. To conjugate the problem of the *mal d'archive,* once again, both as the pathology and as the madness of the repetition compulsion, though in a different manner, con-cerned more with the philosophical and less fixated on the altogether moribund mourning of a philosophical death. On the one hand, all expeditures made to secure a future (for) thinking after the recogni-tion of the impermanence, or *the lack,* of an absolute thought must rely on the aim to "coordinate a single corpus, in a system or a syn-chrony"[5] of repeatable structures, and hence to settle the foundation of a soci-ety, its com-mun-ity, its laws and institutions, what it values and teaches, protects: in short, to *make real* the desire to consum-mate, once again, the hospitality of THE DOMICILE (*oikia*), where "we" could live and *be-at-home-in-being.* On the other, the reconstruc-tion of the ground of the public sphere—the cosmopolitical[6]—is compelled to take place with and against the recesses of memory (*mneme, anamnesis, hypomnema*) after the work of mourning is done, though not yet finished, and provides solace in relief of what the an-archontic, an-archival, tendency toward a dismantling of the system of hierarchical order leaves us open to,[7] *the impression of a "clean break," a breach or rupture, of the history of the archive, of philosophy and its teaching.* The contradiction of attempting to "close off" meta-physics or put it "between brackets" (*entre crochets*),[8] to try to exclude it while still having to retain *ipso facto* the mnemonic trace of its op-erating principles in order to move beyond metaphysics, to OVER-

COME it,[9] soon becomes evident. And so there is a false consciousness of the loss of the archive. Its self-deluding internalization of a
condition of separation as a self-limiting idea supporting the fever of
a mourning for the death of philosophy is destructive, because the
focus is put on *the end* rather than *the closure* of philosophy.[10] There
is no sense of respect for the alterity of what *may* or *could* come after
the prolonged completion of metaphysics, after the trace of repetition
wrought by time and difference. What was inaugurated through the
extended path of the ontological quest to counter the forgetting of
Being sought to bring about its unconcealment (*aletheia*), its unfor-
getting, by attempting to call back into cultural and epistemic memory the conceptualization of the Spirit of Being and its perfected essence, defined after early Greek thinking as the self-presence of
presence totally present to itself.[11] For this well-rounded circularity
was the beginning and the end of philosophy. Tensions between the
"unknowable weight"[12] of competing desires, set to fill the chaos of
the apocalyptic impression of a lack of a secure ground, and hence
the absence of meaning, lead to the seductive awakening of a recon-
structive drive singularly bent toward facilitating a "return to order"
as an escape from a state of *athesis, nonpositionality,* limbo.[13] All of
these words most certainly are synonyms for death, the non-being of
Being, and the *agon* of its metaphysical *aporia*.[14] A denegation of the
genealogy of "the Idea" and its ideo-logy does not recognize, however,
that the legacy of philosophy can never be fully erased from cultural
memory because the *imprimatura* of its diachronic sign traces the bor-
derlines of Western thought on both sides of its dividing line. The
agonia of fighting against the renunciation of that which we desire to
keep close to home because it is familiar (*heimliche*), because it is famil-
iarity itself—where "we" live and dwell—is saturated with the sense
of the need to identify a metalanguage for externalizing the experiential loss of a stable center of meaning in the *syntagmata* of metaphysics, and to facilitate the releasing of an excessive melancholia resulting from the (post)modern subject losing faith in its semiotico-
psychic attachments to an ordered conception of life-world (*Lebens-
welt*) "bit by bit" (*Einzeldurchführung*).[15]

   And yet neither Derrida nor deconstruction—the one not being
the same as the other —has ever acknowledged, called for, or cele-

brated the death of philosophy—if such a thing could indeed be "cele-
brated," welcomed in its popularization. The enclosure of metaphysics in a frame of perfect finitude places restrictions on the possibility
and impossibility of engaging thinking at the outer limits of truth.
And for good reason. Taking the *step/not beyond* (*pas au delà*) philosophy cannot likely be accomplished (from) without philosophy, if it
can be accomplished at all (which is really another way of saying it
cannot). This is the *aporia of passage* that must be negotiated with the
aid of deconstruction and its risky strategy of an *ex-orbit-ant* modality
of reading that marks the double bind of the logic of each and any
attempt to *transgress* or even, in some instances, *arrest* the progress
of metaphysics, whatever this may mean to a future of thinking that
has always already been in a perpetual state of closure and therefore
without end. The route to new forms of knowledge is characterized
by this *ethical* problem of the paradox of the lack of an outside: *paradox,* from its root in the Greek *paradoxon,* meaning a thinking beyond
popular opinion (*doxa*), yet placed within the hyperteleology of duty,
the right (*orthotes*) of what can or cannot be *justly glorified,* deserves
to be held up as an exemplary model to be emulated because it is at
once a singular exception, a rare or impossible occurrence, worthy of
praise, *doxastic.* The law of this antinomy represented by the image of
the "*hors-texte,*" whose double reading Derrida has used to identify
the illusion of exteriority, the *il n'y a pas* of an "out-text" or the non-
presence of an "*outside-of-the-text,*" thus structures the inconsolability
of the mournful desire to *withdraw from* philosophy so as to regain
the essence of subject-ivity and re-claim the Spirit of Being in the
name of difference and its radicalization of heterogeneity: for example, the multitudinal guises of a negative and relational locality actual-
ized by the term "Otherness."[16] And this may seem a strange and perhaps scandalous indictment, especially to those who have struggled
in good faith, yet blindly, to overturn universalism for the purpose of
instating particularity, only to find that via the cultural/material space
of an inscription of identity for its own sake, essentialism quickly dis-
sipates the ethical necessity of recognizing and responding to the alterity of an Other with/in the Selfsame. The struggle to escape metaphysics, however precautionary its measures and forthrightness of
purpose (good faith, ethicity, openness), will always fail outright, be-

cause its closure is by definition interminable, a process of repetition, alterity, a variegation without ending or end. The incommensurability between this lack of an opening and the overzealous push to enforce a moment of finality becomes the enigmatic center of the paradox that suspends philosophy amid mirrored images of its past achievements and the impossible dreams of its future glory. But then, the ethical questioning of the trajectory of metaphysics and its hypergenealogical aftermath, beyond end and closure, still persists. It proceeds mainly along the *peras* or axis of these guiding lines. Questions persist. Is philosophy doomed to pursue in vain the eschatological struggle of attempting to efface the traces of itself so as to break free from the onto-ideologico-epistemic archive of past and present knowledges? To effectively look forward to bringing about its own death in order to recreate itself anew, by seeking to step beyond—and by doing so step/not beyond—the ground of metaphysics and its institutions? Is philosophy without philosophy possible? Desirable? Can there be a closure or/and an end of metaphysics? And would this constitute an ethical crisis for philosophy and its archeo-logical institution that is disseminated and regulated culturally as/in a form of teaching and learning? And what of its pedagogy, *the right of its pedagogy both as form and content?* Who would have the *right to philosophy, to teaching and learning philosophy* (the *right* philosophy?) and its "other heading," the *right of its other heading?*[17] These are no doubt difficult questions. Impossible interrogations, *aporias* we could assuredly call them with some confidence. In relating as they do to the history of philosophy and its institution, these questions I have posed *without precaution* attempt to reiterate and readdress what Derrida identifies—in the propositions from "Violence and Metaphysics: An Essay on the Thought of Emmanuel Levinas" cited at the beginning of this chapter—as the "problems put philosophy as problems philosophy cannot resolve."[18] I must consequently disarm myself of any claims to knowledge presumptuous of "final solutions" and its liberal affectations of a teleological exodus of sorts. The force of the questioning cannot subside, however, and be absorbed in the paralyzing desire for an end-thought, an end to/of thought. Because it simply will not happen that I will solve the riddle of *finding a way out of philosophy.* It would be wiser, and surely ethical enough, to forgo any such analytico-idealistic aspirations from the start, so as to prepare the path for the possibility of an affirmation arising from *within* or *through* the *aporia* of a non-passage, to what may lie beyond the borders of metaphysics yet remains ensconced in the haunt of logocentrism.[19] This disarmament, curiously enough, therefore, also constitutes a necessary precaution, much needed *guardrails* to work against and, if possible, to exceed (Derrida would say), and thereby re-mark the dangerous boundaries of the "limits of truth," where the solid ground of reason gives way to the undecidability of the abyss, an *Ur-ground* perhaps of an-other type, an impossible one, itself being grounded, like deconstruction, in an ungrounding of its groundedness (e.g., presence as absence or lack, neither emptiness nor a void). If I were wholly bound by a finite sense of the debt owed to the scholarly duty of attempting *at all costs* to reach terminal—rather than provisional—conclusions that are intended to "wrap up" research and halt discussion, I would not be predisposed to what may unexpectedly announce itself out of my rereading of another of Derrida's "educational texts" that I have temporarily suspended as I attempt to engage these fundamental questions concerning the "right" of philosophy's birth and death, and the ethics of its body of teaching, also of its teaching body (*corps enseignant*). Still, it is not a matter of throwing all caution to the wind in order to make laudable pronouncements. So, I will proceed according to the caveat Derrida applies to his original presuppositions, and works around, as well as under: "It may even be that these questions are not *philosophical,* are not *philosophy's* questions."[20]

The thought is remarkable. Especially considering the fact that not so dissimilar questions regarding the future of metaphysics have been posed at different times during the recent history of philosophy—in a variety of registers, pitches, and tones, apocalyptic, idealist, and otherwise—by Immanuel Kant and Martin Heidegger, for example.[21] But with Derrida and the deconstruction of logocentrism, we are cognizant of the need to move to new ground now, after and out of the path of idealism and ontology—to proceed ethically with and beyond the debt and duty owed to the archeo-logical excavations of a past time. Only through a responsible questioning that rises out of what is said and left unsaid in the Western tradition of metaphysics can a reaffirmation of "philosophy" as the interpretational moment of a disciplinary line of inquiry, as the translation of an institutional framework, and as the enactment of a pedagogy potentially occur. Derrida—and I have said this before—has consistently tried to make an epistemic shift from ontology and a classical thinking of difference to de-ontology and the affirmative ethics of *différance,* with the help of deconstruction, "an institutional practice for whom the concept of institution remains a problem."[22] The ethical moment of this opening of location and locality, the space and place, *khorismos* and *khora,* from which to engage and facilitate a return to questions of academic responsibility in hopes of transforming the ground of thinking and practice, is vital for what is at stake—that is, for the future of philosophy itself. Despite its wanting "to reach the point of a certain exteriority [non-closure, alterity or otherness] in relation to the totality of the age of logocentrism,"[23] deconstruction nevertheless must remain hopelessly and forever tied to the normative discourse of metaphysics. But it perseveres in taking an affirmative line of questioning with respect to the reductive formulizability of binary thought and its hypersimplistic, teleo-idiomatic construction of the ontological difference of identity in both conceptual and empirical terms. Deconstruction, whether it wants to or not, redefines the conditional determinacy of the axiological limits to thinking that it meets and will ultimately test, so as to converge upon uncharted destinations of thinking, teaching, and learning without the confines of a ready-made (*etymon*), contextualized map, an inalterable archive of "what knowledge is of most worth." Its duty to question what is held sacred, taken for granted as TRUTH (always in boldly capital letters), even venerated, risks both *all* and *nothing* because of its open responsibility to the Other whose effects on the formation of the subject and subjectivity are incalculable. This is what Derrida's careful resigning of deconstruction to a reconsideration of the problems of philosophy that I cited at the start of this chapter entails, implies, signifies. And, of course, dare I say it, more—as we shall see.

WHITHER DECONSTRUCTION? OF PHILOSOPHY FROM THE COSMOPOLITICAL POINT OF VIEW

To address now the "where" of this ethical (re)ground(ing) of deconstruction and the question of the future of philosophy after the unclimactic *apocalypsis* of its multiple and infamous deaths. We must necessarily begin again, this time from a more *"appropriate"* and apoplectic location and locality, yet in a more polemically analytical tone adopted without apologies or a posture of consolation. We need to ask, like Derrida in *The Right to Philosophy from the Cosmopolitical Point of View,* "where, in what place, can a question [of the right to philosophy] take place?"²⁴ Is a location that still occupies the space of philosophy and is at the same time alterior to it possible? For even though we have already started to engage this theme of the necessity of marking the interior and exterior limits of metaphysics without the self-conscious nostalgia of a postmodern pose of mourning the loss of the archive, my reading of Derrida's text will inevitably lead to some judgments about the certainty of "where ought it take place."²⁵ The ethical problem of who is, or should be, capable of determining the propriety of the formal location of inquiry—the space and place of the culturo-institutional indexicality marking the public paths of its entrances and exits—is a flash point of conflict. It implicates deconstruction in the perennial question of democracy and discipline, of excessive delimitations and the archiving of knowledge, and brings us face-to-face, yet again, with the violent opening of the institution of pedagogy and the difference of the Other.

It is in the body of the aforenamed lecture, presented at an international colloquium on philosophy and education hosted by UNESCO, that the qualitative essence of the problematic is translated by Derrida through the open-ended form of an interrogative modality focused (with only a little assistance from me) as follows: "Where does it ['the question of the right to philosophy'] find today its most appropriate place?"²⁶ The readily obvious and easy answer would be, "in the university." But it would be an understatement to say that this response in itself is not enough of a justification for restating the case to uphold what has been an institutional appropriation of the decision-making power and its obligation of accountability with respect to the curricular course of public education. Although this tidy retort—"in the university"—may suffice (and it surely does!) for those who like and are adept at building walls around the right to philosophy as the private property of a select few, the "self-chosen ones," who have the discipline and training to "think" and "do" philosophy "properly," it does not show a love of philosophy, a desire to embrace the asking of questions, as John D. Caputo puts it, "always from a love of what philosophy loves—knowledge and truth (no capitals, please) and ethics and every other honorable and prestigious name in philosophy's intimidating repertoire."[27] The moment of axiomatic interrogation can be taken further to address the academic responsibility of educational institutions, and by extension those who teach, work, and live *in* and, perhaps, *for* them, as this is how the teaching body (*le corps enseignant*) begins and where it ends.[28] What does this mean exactly? To say that a pedagogical institution and those who are a part of it possess total and unabiding—and hence *irresponsible and unaccountable*—control of the intellectual domain they survey is to surmise a legacy of exclusion. There is no space left to welcome another. It is a question of affinity and openness toward embracing the difference of the Other without giving way to hesitation or reservation, empirical qualification and moral judgment, let alone indignation. (The very thought of it! The very idea!) But what does this have to do with philosophy as an institutional discipline, with the curricular organization of its knowledge and its learning, with teaching?

Deconstruction, if it could, would probably answer, "Everything and nothing." But the question of a "proper domain" of the question of rights of institution—of propriety and domination, appropriation, expropriation; of property, participation, ownership, and fairness; and therefore of law, ethics, and ultimately of social justice—brings us back to the proliferative connections to be made between culture and philosophy, and also among *democraticity, governance,* and governmentality, to the responsibilities and principles relating to the formation and formativity of a system of public education on an international scale. It is a matter of locating the axiomatic difference of these terms, the difference of their axiomaticity, and their inter-relatability, within a hospitable space and place that only deconstruction can entreat them to via a hyper-genealogical route of concept excavation eventually leading to a productive recognition of alterity—that is, an ethical expansion of thought and thinking without limitations or borders. Derrida redefines the heterogeneous scope of this impossible territory wherein the struggle over the right to philosophy occurs, after Kant's "risky" envisioning of the cosmopolitical condition: a hypothetical situation of geoglobal interconnectivity or "mondialization" having an "international or interstate dimension"[29] and related to the question of the *emanation* and diaspora of the *poleis* and *politeia as a way of life* by solidifying the problem of a universal history or "a link among the cities, the *poleis* of the world, as nations, as people, or as States."[30] Although, to make it very plain, the deconstructive constellations of this panoptic vision do not harbor the same omniscient hope of confirming the epistemologico-historical foundations of an "abstract universalism"[31] upon which a template for writing the blueprint of any and all institutions *to come* can be inscribed. The interrogative modality of this desire for a re-thinking of the future of thinking works toward illuminating and transforming rather than dismissing or deriding the historicity of "philosophical acts and archives."[32] Deconstruction, in questioning the ground of institutions and the reason of their institutionality, engages the real-world effects produced by the performative force of epistemological discourses, and their responsibility as instances of founding and therefore of foundation. Its anti-utopian thrust, however contrary to the ideal of a natural universalism of thought and action uniting thinking and subjectivity in the image of the global citizen, nevertheless enables Derrida to conjoin the problem of the right to philosophy with the Kantian conception of a cosmopolitical point of view in a positive rather than a negative way. Here we must acknowledge something parenthetical, something bracketed because it is more literally "literary" than prophetic, though not to be ignored. The title of Derrida's lecture alludes to *Idea (in View) of a Universal History from a Cosmopolitical Point of View (Idee zu einer allgemeinen Geschichte in weltbürgerlicher Absicht)*, one of an

> ensemble of Kant's writings that can be described as *announcing*, that is to say, predicting, prefiguring, and prescribing a certain number of international institutions that only came into existence (*qui n'ont vu le jour*) in this century, for the most part after the Second World War. These institutions are already *philosophemes*, as is the idea of international law or rights that they attempt to put into operation.[33]

The intertextual association sets the tone for a rereading of the reading of the event and its surroundings, which Derrida performs then and there. It reauthorizes the focus on recognizing the legitimacy of UNESCO as "the privileged place"[34] for asking the question of the right to philosophy from a cosmopolitical point of view. And the contextual markers of the lecture—to whom it is addressed and why (for what purpose, effect, reason, and so on)—compel us toward a consideration of what Derrida defines as "two types of relation"[35] involving the university and the politico-cultural grounding of the human sciences:

1. The *international* relation among universities or research institutes on the one hand, and among international institutions of culture (governmental or non-governmental) on the other;
2. The particular *interdisciplinary* relation between [*sic*] philosophy, the arts, the sciences, and the "humanities." "Philosophy" names here both a discipline that belong to the "humanities" and the discipline that claims to think, elaborate, and criticize the axiomatic of the "humanities," particularly the problem of the humanism or the presumed universalism of the "humanities."[36]

Relative to the situational dynamics of the discursive presentation of the lecture itself, the reference is multiplied in its associations and disassociations by its applicability to the unique case of UNESCO. An institution of the postwar era "perhaps born from the positing (*la position*) of a right to philosophy from the cosmopolitical point of view,"[37] it imbibes in its constitutional commitments and formal configurations "an assignable *philosophical history*" that "impl[ies] sharing a culture and a philosophical language."[38] That is, it implies the exchange of a tradition of knowledge and knowing as articulated by the continual re-aggregation of the logic of the letter, the terms of its reading as production and reproduction, and the domain of its archive. The problem of how to go about securing both private and public access to this language and culture, "first and foremost by means of education,"[39] involves, more or less, the working-out of the "two types of relation" Derrida identifies as being central to answering the question of academic privilege (who has the right to philosophy?) and the power of location (how and why?). The pedagogical onus on an affable (simple, crude, vulgar) modality of cultural production and reproduction, without the complexity of resistance or complications, fixes the parameters of an institutional ethic of response and responsibility. But this reduction of the frame of reference to categorical imperatives that willfully ignore the limitations and boundaries of a project of repeating the historicity of Western education occurs only if and when the cosmopolitical nature of UNESCO is not taken into account. For it would be wrong to ignore the diversity within its composition and to call this institution an academicized model of universalism without difference. Derrida explains the emanation of the cosmopolitical view—and its gathering of multiplicity—through the image of a charter (constitution, treaty, settlement, founding document, statement of rights and obligations, laws, etc.), so as to underscore the implications of the covenant of relation UNESCO enacts by involving a contractual obligation between philosophy and action that articulates the ethical terms of its responsibility:

> All the States that adhere to the charters of these international institutions [like UNESCO, the United Nations also] commit themselves, in principle, *philosophically*, to recognize and put into operation in an effective way something like philosophy and a certain philosophy of rights and law, the rights of man [sic], universal history, etc. The signature of these charters is a philosophical act that makes a commitment to philosophy in a way that is philosophical. From that moment on, whether they say so or not, know it or not, or conduct themselves accordingly or not, these States and these peoples, by reason of their joining (*par leur adhésion*) these charters or participating in these institutions, contract a philosophical commitment—therefore, at the very least, a commitment to provide the philosophical culture or education that is required for understanding and putting into operation these commitments made to the international institutions, which are, I repeat, philosophical in essence.[40]

An organization of many parts and partners—nations, states, and peoples whose materiality comprises and cannot but exceed the conceptual totality of its essence—UNESCO "bears both the response and responsibility for this question"[41] of the right to philosophy, and for a reconsideration of the obligation to unite response with responsibility within the milieu of the international and interdisciplinary institution of the university and other places of research it represents by virtue of its associations. The "very form of this question concerning a question (*au sujet d'une question*)—namely 'where, in what place, can a question take place?' "[42]—implies both complementary and contradictory assumptions, also judgments. On the one hand can be found the need for an adjudication of the legitimacy of the opportunity given or taken to respond to the question of the right to philosophy and the determination of its "most appropriate place," its most "proper" location. On the other, it goes directly to evaluating the quality of the response. But these aspects are not unrelated, insofar as such ethico-qualitative judgments also make necessary an identification of who would have the privilege and opportunity of participation in curricular decisions about the future of the philosophical discipline, and why. We shall get to this a little bit later. It is enough to say now that this will lead us toward the impossibility of the future of UNESCO, and to the global diaspora of philosophy education. That is, to the institutional interconnections of a *democracy-to-come* with a *pedagogy-to-come*, and the potentially diverging paths of its filiations and friendships—what is held close, in affinity, to the spirit and the heart, not the mind.

But going back once again to the image of UNESCO as the overriding reality and symbol (the objective correlative?) of what "would thus, perhaps fundamentally, be the privileged place"[43] for asking the question of the right to philosophy. The necessity of its very existence, certainly less than fate but more than chance, enjoins us to inquire after the historicity of the institution and its ideo-ground from the Kantian delineation of the cosmopolitical point of view. This is easily justified by Derrida:

> one would say that there are places *where there are grounds* for asking this question. That is to say, that here this question is legitimately and rightfully not only possible and authorized but also necessary, indeed prescribed. In such places, such a question—for example, that of the right to philosophy from the cosmopolitical point of view—can and should take place.[44]

By citing the grounds of a deconstructive propriety, Derrida prepares the way to radically modify the idealist presupposition of a "plan of nature that aims at the total, perfect political unification of the human species (*die vollkommene bürgerliche Vereinigung in der Menschengattung*)"[45] through the unfolding of the history of the transcendental unity of the Idea. Kant's ethical universalism, and its infamous Eurocentric bias, is used in a novel way: it is turned toward the question of the right to philosophy to mobilize the cosmopolitical as a viewpoint not only for reconceptualizing the "eternal becoming"[46] of being-in-the-world, *but as a new approach to realizing the impossible futures of a "progressive institutionality" to come and the unforeseeability of its educational methods and apparatus.* This does not simply mean a securing of the opportunity for freedom in thinking and teaching; neither does it defer pedagogically or ethically to the teaching of thinking without reference to the tradition of Western episteme, however it may be defined in curricular terms. I have emphasized this earlier. Derrida cites the Kantian notion of *the cosmopolitical* to reawaken and to resituate the Eurocentrism of the concept and its implications for reinscribing the "horizon of a new community"[47] (of the question and the impossibility of the question) that teaches the Other to question the sources of the Self and the Other. This may sound strange to those who envision and portray deconstruction as a *destruction* of Western metaphysics, its institutions and its teachings. We need to remember, however, the case of UNESCO as an institution that is *a priorii* "Kantian in spirit."[48] Which is to say, it *predicts* a Western trajectory of thinking along a "teleological axis"[49] with respect to the epistemologico-cultural ideal of the "infinite progress" of Being and the temporal procession of beings toward perfectibility, achievable or not. Anything else "would be nothing but a novel," given the inseparability of the European history of philosophy from the notion of the universal. As Derrida explains,

> Whoever would have doubts about such a unification and above all about a plan of nature, would have no reason to subscribe even to the fact of sharing a philosophical problematic, of a supposedly universal or universalizable problematic of philosophy. For anybody having doubts about this plan of nature, the whole project of writing a uni-

versal—and therefore philosophical—history, and thus as well the
project of creating institutions governed by an international—and
therefore philosophical—law, would be nothing but a novel.[50]

An institution is founded on memory and the material conditions of
its working-out as a dynamic tradition of theory and practice, philosophy and action. Derrida recognizes this and has never denied it. In
fact, I would say his work of deconstruction is predicated *on taking
memory into account*: accounting for the causality of its effects, its
bias, its exclusions—rendering an account of what makes memory,
disrupts it, constructs its limits and openings, how and why it favors.
To bring the analysis back to the text we are rereading, UNESCO as
an international institution is founded on the principles of European
philosophy, its charter and its concepts "are philosophical through
and through"[51]—which does not make them universal in scope or essence, despite the reality that UNESCO does attempt to influence,
"for the better," the educational landscape of the world-picture. This
latter point is important in reading the dimensions of the first. That
the aim of this organization is, in theory, altruistic cannot be denied,
as the logic of its existence is predicated, in principle, on the presupposition of the idea of an infinite perfectibility of human being. It
mobilizes a thoroughly Western conceit and philosophical project directed toward the rectification of Being as presence and the sending
of itself forward in time. For Derrida, it is not a matter of questioning
the existence of UNESCO outside of the scope of its mission statement and the theoretical grounds of the practical action laid out by
the logic of its charter. In ethical, philosophical, and real-world
terms, we can easily justify the necessity of its "being-there" on an
international, global scale, especially when considering that its charter upholds a cosmopolitical model of membership, governance, and
responsibility for decision making, sanctioning the development and
sustenance of democratic means and conditions for securing public
access to education. It would not make sense to dismiss or defame
UNESCO either as an instrument of Western influence and cogitation
or as an indicator of the extent of Western domination across the
hemispheres with respect to propagating a "certain philosophy of
rights and law, the rights of man [sic], universal history,"[52] and so on.

A critique—coming down on one side or the other—of its efficacy is not at all useful, but a misleading endeavor seeking an ethical refuge in the evaluative power of a binary form of metaphysical reasoning that pits "the good" against "the bad," "essentialism" against "anti-essentialism," "Eurocentrism" against "anti-Eurocentrism," and so on. The endwork of a critical task that freely places blame or adjudicates value for the sake of a castigation or rejection of worth is performed too quickly and easily. Its decisions are rendered by and appeal to the dictates of a universalist conception of "reason" and its demotic (and not at all democratic) corollary of "common sense" to construct the ideologico-conceptual grounds of what is "good" and what is "bad." The judgmental edifice of its either/or rationale presumes a lack of interpretative complexity, a plainness of truth that is totally transparent and obvious to everyone, a clear-cut and unarguable judgment made with no room to fathom the possibility of opposition or exemption to the rule of law. One life-world. One reality. One Truth. The metaphysical value of this ethic of perception and its monological model of representation determines the nonoppositional grounds of truth. Conditional and definitive limits thereby demarcate the freedom of what it is possible to know, think, and say without offending the much guarded sensibilities of "reason" and "good taste"—however their values might be constructed and articulated—as the ideals of commonly held responses to cultural institutions and practices. Difference is abdicated in favor of a community of shared interpretative responsibility and the unethical hegemony of its "majority rules" attitude that bids one to erect barriers against diversity, "to see and talk about things only as they are or could be." For the priority of clarity as an ethical prerequisite of a "responsible response" is, without a doubt, everything when the analytical imperative is nothing but an exercise of choosing sides. There is a more productive approach, nevertheless, that would open up the possibility of reaffirming the utility and necessity of UNESCO as a cosmopolitical institution by recontextualizing the conditions of its founding to the "new situation"[53] of the present day, without having to tear down the conceptual frame of its material structures in order to set up something else that would reproduce and multiply the faults of the original. What would this involve? Deconstruction, of course!

Derrida provides a way to begin reassessing and reaffirming the responsibilities of UNESCO in relation to the demands and conditions of a "new international" by opening up the logic of its existence as a "world institution" concerned with the problem of global education to the question of the right to philosophy and its teaching:

> What are the concrete stakes of this situation today? Why should the large questions of philosophical teaching and research, and the imperative of the right to philosophy, be developed more than ever in their international dimension? Why are the responsibilities to be assumed no longer simply national, less national today than ever, and even less tomorrow than ever, in the twenty-first century? What do "national," "international," "cosmopolitical," and "universal" signify here, for and with regard to philosophy, philosophical research, philosophical education or training, and indeed for a philosophical question or practice that would not be essentially linked to research or education?[54]

The questions are succinct and precise; in looking forward to a *future-to-come* they go right to the heart of the childhood age of philosophy and education—"specifically European, specifically Greek"[55] in its origins—that spawned the possibility and impossibility of UNESCO in the first place. Derrida does not call for an uncritical rejection of the memory of the institution, the conceptual history of the institution's memory, its *Begriffsgeschichte*, and so avoids the consequences of what Kant feared most: a non- or antiphilosophical development of human being and its institutions. A disturbing implication follows, as it both inaugurates and repeats the classical divisions of Eurocentrism by distinguishing those who are perceived to have civilization and those who supposedly do not—essentially, by providing the ethico-logical and historico-epistemic basis for differentiating between the sources of a Western culture and the "errant traditions" of its Others. This "guiding thread of a pattern of nature"[56] that Kant identifies, and the Occidentalism of its cosmopolitical trajectory, takes this history, "first of all in its Greek, and then Roman, beginnings, in opposition to the so-called barbaric nations."[57] A condemning statement. A "convenient instrument of representation (*Darstellung*),"[58] Derrida calls it, this uncomplicated identification of a "guiding thread." The affective influence of its trace demarcates and legitimizes the general culture of a Western subjectivity as the only "authentic" mode of *being-in-the-world,* distinct from and prior to its alien Others. "This is why," Derrida says, "this text [of Kant's], which is cosmopolitical in spirit, according to a law that could be verified well beyond Kant, is the most strongly Eurocentered text that can be, not only in its philosophical axiomatic but also in its retrospective reference to Greco-Roman history and in its prospective reference to the future hegemony of Europe which, Kant says, is the continent that 'will probably legislate some day for all the others.'"[59] Again, it would be too easy, perfunctory, and without forethought to leave the analysis there. And, as can be expected, Derrida does not. UNESCO cannot be viewed simply as a political *organon* that represents and wields the interests and power of a Western intellectual imperialism obsessed with promoting its own archival essence at the expense of an Other that it performatively inheres, and therefore *appropriates,* as part of the axiomatics and axiology of its governing charter. This negative aspect of its institutional history and historicity cannot be denied, given its Eurocentric response and responsibility: the "rational ruse"[60] of its origins as a union of nations, states, and peoples of "equal partnership" but of unequal participation, voice, power, and representation. Derrida makes numerous references to Kant's text and copiously documents the implications it inheres and therefore exemplifies about the cultural domination of the cosmopolitical reality, viewpoint, or condition by Western Europe, a "continent (*in unserem Weltteile*) (which will probably legislate one day for all other continents [*der wahrscheinlicher Weise allen anderen dereinst Gesetz geben wird*])."[61]

This is familiar territory, though not because I have re-cited the quotation in order to reiterate and augment its importance. The ethical impetus of the "postcolonial," "anticolonial," or even the "neocolonial" moment (as Gayatri Chakravorty Spivak calls it) begins with a philosophical nod to what is, for Derrida, the legacy of the institutions and models of "Greco-European memory."[62] Addressing the textual composition of this epistemic and cultural genealogy of Western knowledge, Kant's discourse is only one example of a host of writings by philosophers who possess the temerity to have made such audacious and largely accurate statements about the dominance of "the guiding thread (*Leitfaden*) of Greek history (*griechische Geschichte*)"[63] with respect to explaining the unfolding of the Reason of Being across space and over time. The axiomaticity of this logic directed at excluding an Other from the fundamental (pure) archive of its heritage would be only natural from a philosophical perspective of human historicity that narcotizes the productive value of difference and thus disallows the possibility of heterogeneous opening to a world community from a cosmopolitical point of view. As Derrida says, "One encounters [its Eurocentric axiology] again and again, intact and invariable throughout variations as serious as those that distinguish Hegel, Husserl, Heidegger, and Valéry."[64] But of course there is a difference in what Kant proposes by way of a vision of the world from a cosmopolitical point of view and its universal enactment in the form of a "Society of Nations," despite the emphasis he places upon Greek philosophy and history, because it attempts to *sublate*, to synthesize and at the same time keep, the tensions of the values of cultural difference in an amicable and moral unification of humanity worked out, more or less, along the trajectory of the "teleological axis of this discourse [that] has become the tradition of European modernity."[65] The concept of nature, and specifically the "unsociability (*Ungeselligkeit, Unvertragsamkeit*)"[66] of human being *by nature*, is actually the means to a salvation "through culture, art and artifice (*Kunst*), and reason, to make the seeds of nature blossom."[67] And Kant truly believes in the potentially unifying power of this "natural or originary state of war among men"[68] (again Derrida's word, and it is quite appropriate here, for in Kant's time there could literally only be a state of war *among men*). Because of the propensity of subjective (cultural) differences to force antagonisms, territoriality, and conflict, there is only one possible solution: "That which resembles a novel-like story yet isn't one, that which in truth is but the very historicity of history . . . this ruse of nature."[69] And here we may be amazed by how Kant's text embellishes and reveals the philosophical historicity of UNESCO:

> Nature has thus again used the unsociability (*Ungeselligkeit, Unvertragsamkeit*) of men, and even the unsociability among the large soci-

eties and political bodies which human beings (*créatures*) construct and are given to, as a means of forging a state of calm and security from their inevitable antagonism. Thus the excessive and unremitting military preparations for war, and the resultant misery which every state must eventually feel within itself, even in the midst of peace, are the means by which nature drives nations to make initially imperfect attempts: but only, after many devastations, upheavals and even complete inner exhaustion of their powers, to take the step which reason could have suggested to them even without so many sad experiences—that of abandoning a lawless state of savagery and entering a Society of Nations of peoples in which every state, even the smallest, could expect to derive its security and rights not from its own power or its own legal judgment, but solely from this great Society of Nations [of peoples: *Völkerbunde*] (*foedus amphyctionum*), from a united power and the law-governed decisions of a united will.[70]

Violence—and its threat to the security of human *Dasein*—is the catalyst that allows nature "to aid reason and thereby put philosophy into operation through (*à travers*) the society of nations."[71] For Derrida, this is a troubling but understandable sublating (*relever*) of the antitheses holding together the diffuse logic of the global cosmopolitical community. On the one hand, peace achieved through the danger of violence is not really a peace made at all. It is a provisional state of human entropy with respect to the appeasement of the tensions of difference and the possible eruption of transgressions and aggressions against subjective alterity; it depends on the ethico-philosophical essence of the cosmopolitical covenant of being. The condition of peace represents the satiating of an impulse to nullify the difference of difference. On the other hand, a peace compelled by the dark side of the human spirit is perhaps the only *possible and natural* peace that could be rendered effective or legislated, when no other decision or action is acceptable, viable, or defensible given the alternative of violence. This of course begs the question of the constitutive force of community—whatever that IDEAL may entail as an affective identification of a subjective sense of belonging, a *being-at-home-in-the-world WITH OTHERS*—and the responsibility of its opening-up of the Self unto the difference of the Other. When these two states or conditions of existence, peace (community) and violence (war), are placed in direct opposition to each other, the ethical choice is clearly delineated by the power of a humanistic appeal to a *universal* and hence *moral will* denying the propriety of any transgression of subjectivity at all costs, even if this means suppressing human rights and freedoms for "the greater good." Community, then, is a matter of instilling and practicing a homogeneous concept of culture, a *general* culture whose model of a collective intersubjectivity acts as a unified resistance to the threat of alterity. The promoting of common points of recognition and identification within the ideologico-philosophical consciousness of its constituents, in order to defy or suppress the propensity for violence against the threat of difference—or at the very least to quell the performativity of the desire to do so—establishes the psychic and figural ground for the foundations of friendship and belonging. Following the determinative ethics of these rules of consensus in the name of community and commonality (and also of communication) reduces the Other to the Same and minimizes the potential of a subjective resistance to the inclusion of contrariety within a closed system of shared associations. This illusion of unity masks the radical violence of alterity and softens the risk of its provisional acceptance by replacing the shock of its reality with the comforting image of a single, harmonious group, a majority without difference. *They is Us.* The correlation of subjectivity relieves the discord of diversity because one has to inhere and adhere to the fundamental agreements of a consensual state of abstract universalism in order to be part of the general (yet specific) culture of a community. *I am We.* An ethical and philosophical contrition of sorts must be achieved in this case by the subject, to ensure a "responsible response" that is itself a coming to peace of the Self with the avowable laws of a community and its effacing of difference.

If we consider the Eurocentrism of the reasoning Kant puts forward for pursuing a universal alliance of humanity from the cosmopolitical view, and its prefiguring of new models of global gathering and world institutions like the United Nations and UNESCO, we cannot avoid addressing the ethico-philosophical focus of such an idea aimed at rearticulating the notion of community. The appeal made to the "higher value" and "intrinsic right" of "Greek historicity or historiographicity"[72] is an attempt to formalize the vision of the endless progression of being toward its positive ethical articulation in "the good life." To avoid the Hegelian nightmare of a "bad" or "poor infinity" (*schlechte Unendlichkeit*)[73] that does not realize the Reason of the History of itself in a dialectical resolution of identity, it becomes quite essential to provide the teleology of an *a priori* epistemic framework "to contradict this novel-like hypothesis [of an international community from a cosmopolitical point of view] and to think human history, beyond the novel, as a system and not as an aggregate without a plan and program, without providence."[74] For Kant, the living memory of Greek philosophy and culture—whether it be *in and of itself* or appropriated, as it eventually was, by Roman thinking—is "the only one in which all other earlier or contemporary histories are preserved and passed on, or at least authenticated."[75] Again, the subsumption of all humanity under the ideological framework of institutions that are the product of a Western European historicity cannot be an innocent and happy coincidence. Surely, this summation could not fail to be the clever fabulation of a novel (*Roman*). To protect against the danger of "the becoming-literature of philosophy,"[76] which Kant so desperately feared would lead human nature astray by inhibiting Being's potential to actualize the intentional apperception of the idea of transcendence and its ideal of infinite progress, there was only one path that could bring beings toward the fulfillment of Reason—"the living thread of Greek history."[77] Derrida explains the "paradoxical incitement"[78] of the judgment—for example, the oppositional conclusions it ultimately leads to regarding whom it excludes, what it privileges, why, where, and how:

> in this teleological ruse of nature, Greco-Roman Europe, philosophy and Occidental history, and I would even dare saying continental history, are the driving force, capital, and exemplary, as if nature, in its rational ruse, had assigned Europe this special mission: not only that of founding history as such, and first of all as science, not only that of founding philosophy as such, and first of all as science, but also the mission of founding a rational philosophical (non-novel-like) history and that of "legislating some day" for all other continents.[79]

The Eurocentrism of the utopia that Kant champions also predicts the creation of organizations such as UNESCO, because the philosophical enactment of its promise of a state of lasting peace is what motivates the impossible achievement of persuading its members to nonviolently surrender their individual autonomy to the security of the collective, essentially by "contracting artificial and institutional links, and . . . entering a Society of Nations."[80] Even so, the question cannot but remain: Why? What privileges Greek history—"history both in the sense of *Geschichte* and *Histoire,* history in the sense of event and of narrative, of the authenticated account, of historical science"[81]—to mediate and guide the future of a cosmopolitical unification of all humanity? The argument comes back, full circle, to what is called "philosophy" and "who" has a right to it, why, where, in what place? The question of the right to philosophy is also a question of the *right* philosophy.

IMPOSSIBLE HORIZONS AND OTHER HEADINGS: OF DEMOCRACY, COMMUNITY, AND THE RIGHT TO PHILOSOPHY

Tempering what we already know, perhaps always have known, with what we discovered or invented along the way—to learn more about what we do not, cannot, know—we must come back to the scenarios we started with to hypothesize the impossible state of a future of thinking after metaphysics. Having worked through a patient reading to arrive at this destination, we are now ready—in light of the cosmopolitical point of view and the case of UNESCO, whose "mode of being is one that is *a priori* philosophical"[82]—to attempt an answer to the irreconcilable nature of the original problems from the opening of "Violence and Metaphysics" that I have used as an epigraph to this chapter. We will have to remind ourselves why Derrida insists "these should be the only questions today capable of founding the community, within the world, of those who are still called philosophers,"[83] which is, of course, everyone and not everyone. Three points are worth further elaboration. All pertain to the critical issue of *how deconstruction can help us to untangle, demystify, transgress the limits and limitations of the aporia of the death of philosophy, and to resolve the question of its question, and of its right, its institution—as well as the question of who has the right and responsibility to respond to it. And why.*

The first point concerns the postmetaphysical horizons of community, both public and academic. For Derrida, it is not a simple matter of *fighting against the pronouncement of the death of philosophy, even though it may be a premature burial*—or so we would like to, and have to, think. To try to resist what is posed as the end of metaphysics by mounting arguments against the finality of this perspective, in the tradition of a "critique" or "negative determination"[84] that seeks its own affirmation through the violence of opposition, is a wasted effort. "A philosopher is always someone for whom philosophy is not *given*, someone who in essence must question the self about the essence and destination of philosophy;"[85] which is to say, the alterity of metaphysics as well as the power of its teleology is always close at hand, whether or not a transcendence of its logic *ever takes place* or *can even happen*—essentially, whether or not it *is possible*. Questions about the end of philosophy, and thus the end of the historicity of history, still abound. Some pose more productive challenges than others to the question, "What, if anything, comes next?" Nevertheless, a sense of community is (oddly enough, some may say) formed around the asking of the question of the end or the death of philosophy. And this is to be expected, when the point is just to a Heideggerian *overcoming* (*Überwindung*) of metaphysics. It is the responsibility of each individual to interrogate the limits of "a sort of axiomatic, a system of values, norms and regulating principles" that justify "the existence . . . of a properly philosophical space and place like UNESCO."[86] Derrida warns that "such a situation and such a duty are more particular than they seem, and this can lead to redoubtable practical consequences,"[87] such as the temptation to take a stance on one side or the other of philosophy, *with* or *against* those who desire to remember and keep alive its memory or those who choose to forget the historicity of metaphysics and forswear the finality of its death. "A community of the question about the possibility of the question"[88] is what Derrida calls the publicly academic space of a more productive ground of inquiry into the right to philosophy than one of either support or diffidence. Such a community would neither reject nor embrace the Eurocentric historicity of Western thinking and its epistemico-cultural specificity, articulated via humanism as the infinite perfectibility of subjective being: the finding of the NATURE OF THE SELF and its center at the cost of losing affinity with the Other. It could not reject or embrace this historicity, because it is a "community of the question"—a community wrought of dissensus and not of consensus. Its potential lies in the openness of its capacity to honor and respect the value of difference: to welcome the impossibility of alterity, but not to dismiss or celebrate the ground of *au courant* memory for its own sake, over the unfamiliar archive of another. So, rather than dismantling the arguments of those who would like to see the demise of the right to philosophy and its Eurocentric historicity, Derrida has attempted to answer and is continuing to address the larger question of the death of metaphysics and of its future, both directly and obliquely, because none of the answers posited as yet do justice to the persistent problem of *finding a way out of philosophy.* Certainly, there is an *aporia* at work here that seeks refuge in its displacement. Derrida construes its difficulty in the following way:

> This Eurocentric discourse forces us to ask ourselves . . . whether today our reflection concerning the unlimited extension and the reaffirmation of a right to philosophy should not both *take into account and de-limit* the assignation of philosophy to its Greco-European origin or memory. At stake is neither contenting oneself with reaffirming a certain history, a certain memory of origins or of Western history of philosophy (Mediterranean or Central European, Greco-Roman-Arab or Germanic), nor contenting oneself with being opposed to, or opposing denial to, this memory and these languages, but rather trying to displace the fundamental schema of this problematic by going beyond the old, tiresome, worn-out, and wearisome opposition between Eurocentrism and anti-Eurocentrism.
>
> One of the conditions for getting there—and one won't get there all of a sudden in one try, it will be the effect of a long and slow historical labor that is under way—is the active becoming-aware of the fact that philosophy is no longer determined by a program, an originary language or tongue whose memory it would suffice to recover so as to discover its destination. Philosophy is no more assigned to its origin or by its origin, than it is simply, spontaneously, or abstractly cosmopolitical or universal. That which we have lived and

what we are more and more aiming for are modes of appropriation and transformation of the philosophical in non-European languages and cultures. Such modes of appropriation and transformation amount neither to the classical mode of appropriation—that consists in making one's own what belongs to the other (here, in interiorizing the Western memory of philosophy and in assimilating it in one's own language)—nor to the invention of new modes of thought, which, as alien to all appropriation, would no longer have any relation to what one believes one recognizes under the name of philosophy.[89]

No discourse or "disciplined" body of knowledge claiming epistemic status, such as philosophy is and does, *self-consciously* undermines its grounding conceits in both methodology and content. The principle of noncontradiction forbids it. What governs the institutional legitimacy of philosophy as a *scientific endeavor* is its ability to render the logic of its conclusions accountable *to* and *for* the provisions of episteme laid out by the historicity of its own doctrines of self-evident truth and the generalizability of conclusions regarding the study of empirical phenomena: what its discourse says and reveals, confirms and proves by way of an experiential facticity, about *being-in-the-world*. In this respect, an ethical moment attends the academic pursuit of knowledge. It occurs when thinking becomes *like a science*, becomes "philosophy," is conceived as a universal project, inaugurates a discipline replete with models of practice to be guarded, and is not defined idiosyncratically as the general process of thought. This distinction, besides giving credence to the institutional and pedagogical formalization and formulizability of the human intellect for and within the structures of the modern university, remains highly problematic. The division between "philosophy and *Denken*, thinking,"[90] reenforces the ethico-epistemic specificity of academic responsibility by setting down the template for marking out the limits of the paragon of a community (to be) instituted, whereby the laws it creates ultimately support and mobilize a dividing line that distinguishes those "who belong" to it from those "who do not" and, in all probability, never will. The partisanship of discipline and disciplinarity plays upon the need for philosophy to be affiliated with the historicity of a "culture." Here we must give way to caution, though, and not presume to know too much. "There are cultural aspects of philosophy," Derrida maintains, "but philosophy is not a cultural phenomenon." What does this mean, exactly, in both the narrow and broader sense of a community of shared and differing interests?

This brings us to the second point. To say that philosophy is a cultural phenomenon would be to universalize it, to deny "the relationship between philosophy and natural languages, European languages"[91]—living and breathing languages that are proper to and establish the propriety of philosophy as an invention of the consciousness of the West and the articulation of its archive. And Derrida is sufficiently clear about this undeniable linguistic historicity, while attempting "to avoid the opposition between two symmetrical temptations, one being to say . . . that . . . philosophy is . . . universal":

> Today it's a well-known phenomenon—there is a Chinese philosophy, a Japanese philosophy, and so on and so forth. That's a contention I would resist. I think there is [too much] specifically European, specifically Greek in philosophy to simply say that philosophy is something universal. . . . Philosophy is a way of thinking. It's not science. It's not thinking in general. So when I say, well, philosophy has some privileged relationship with Europe, I don't say this Eurocentrically, but to take [history seriously].[92]

The closure of philosophy does not mean a gathering together of the Greco-European reality of its roots and forcefully bringing them to an end that would lack any semblance of historicity. The breakthrough of *what-is-to-come* must always arise out of the resources of a past thinking that cannot be effectively renounced. The trace of Greco-European cultural memory in philosophy will allow itself neither to be eradicated nor abandoned at the limit of the archive of knowledge it *is* and *represents* in method, form, and content. This first "temptation" leads to the second, both contrary and complementary: the desire to say, "Well, philosophy has only one origin, a single pure origin that is its foundation, its institution, through a number of grounding concepts which are linked to Greek language, and we have to keep this in memory and constantly go back to Greece and back to this Greek origin—European [origin]—through anamnesis, through memory, to what philosophy is."[93] The Eurocentric myopia of this monocultural view of the archive of Western episteme is another peril of taking sides without actualizing sufficient precautions against the irresponsibility of academic solipsism. Magnifying the question of the historicity of philosophy and of the purity of its Greek origins, this temptation foreshadows the necessity of moving beyond the concept of a universal thought and recognizing the rise of the cosmopolitical condition that Kant predicted as a moment in the infinite process of eternal becoming, or the point in history where a giant step in the progress of humanity can be seen resulting from an outgrowth of the global self-awareness and situatedness of human being. Derrida stresses the virtues of "another model" whose approach to truth cannot be distilled quite so easily into a program of "Eurocentrism and simple-minded anti-Eurocentrism":

> that is, while keeping in memory this European, Greek origin of philosophy, and the European history of philosophy, [to] take into account that there are events, philosophical events, which cannot be reduced to this single origin, and which meant that the origin itself was not simple, that the phenomena of hybridization, of graft, or translation, was there from the beginning. So we have to analyze the different philosophical events today, in Europe and outside of Europe.[94]

In essence, the attempt to make philosophy live out its future after the historicity of its Greco-European past, requires the space of an *aporia*

> that cannot be locked into this fundamentally cultural, colonial, or neocolonial dialectic of appropriation and alienation. There are other ways for philosophy than those of appropriation as expropriation (to lose one's memory by assimilating the memory of the other, the one being opposed to the other, as if an *ex-appropriation* were not possible, indeed the only possible chance).[95]

Derrida is right. The testimony of memory and its reaffirming of an ethical response and responsibility to the historicity of the past is important for inscribing and building the "horizon of a new community."⁹⁶ It is not a matter of reasonable speculation: as the "speculative moment within the academy" will not do justice to rethinking the new situation of nations and states, of peoples, that must "transform their assumptions" in relation to what we now know is the urgent necessity of "displacing some concepts which are absolutely essential to th[e] constitutions"⁹⁷ of international institutions like the United Nations and UNESCO. The cosmopolitical hybridization of empirical and epistemic identity Derrida speaks of does not involve trying to erase the history of one's own memory by working (in vain) to appropriate the effects and affectivity of another archive—the archive of an Other. Nor does it imply making an attempt to start over without history, to efface the contextual and institutional specificity of subjectivity through a haphazard rejection of the philosophical grounding of one's sense of *being-in-the-world*. On the one hand, a rethinking of "Eurocentrism *and* anti-Eurocentrism" as "symptoms of a colonial and missionary culture"⁹⁸ would facilitate other beginnings and other directions for the infinite progress of human being. On the other, "a concept of the cosmopolitical still determined by such opposition would not only still concretely limit the development of the right to philosophy but also would not even account for what happens in philosophy."⁹⁹ Do we have any chance of respecting a desire to promote and protect the call for either the appropriation (expropriation) or ex-appropriation of Western metaphysics on a global and international scale?

If philosophy could ever hope to overcome the impossible dream of achieving its own end, it would be precisely through a curious rupturing of the idea of its historicity, the memory of its *being-past*, which, of course, could never happen. And we should not want an expunging of the history of philosophy, if it were even possible. Metaphysics does not have to be forcefully sedated, sanitized, and subdued. Also, we do not have to issue a proclamation that would render it alive or sentence it to death. As Derrida observes,

> Not only are there other ways for philosophy, but philosophy, if there is any such thing, is the other way.
> And it has always been the other way[.]¹⁰⁰

To be unequivocal, philosophy "has always been bastard, hybrid, grafted, multilinear, and polyglot."[101] The teaching body of the discipline has always known this to be true.[102] Pedagogical systems highlighting methods of recitation and repetition in the delivery of its curriculum were designed as a defense against a mnemonic underdetermination of the totality and authenticity of the philosophical archive (by this I mean the competing models and systems of the reason of Western episteme that explicate the ontological sources of human consciousness and being). What signals the "crisis of philosophy" and leads to a questioning of the value of its teaching and learning—thereby feeding the naive illusion of its untimely demise—are the metaconditional links of possibility: to be more specific, the *conditions of impossibility* within its complex lineage that work to destabilize the history of philosophy and, consequently, open up the concept of philosophy to what is not "philosophy proper" or "proper to philosophy." It is this realization of an originary difference always already present within the writing of its archive that displaces and dislocates its authority to signify and *speak for* the truth of itself. The immutable trace of the difference of an Other thoroughly permeates the historicity of Western knowledge, for "philosophy has never been the unfolding responsible for a unique, originary assignation linked to a unique language or to the place of a sole people. Philosophy does not have a sole memory."[103]

We will now consider the third point. The working within and against a tradition of canonical associations wrought by the instauration of memory and the limitations of its capacity—exemplified in the act of forgetting (*lethe*)—brings out the tensions of disassociation and dissonance that redefine the path of metaphysics. To achieve a spatial and temporal closure of "first philosophy" involves a segue to something *other than philosophy, a thinking of philosophy lacking philosophy*, where "we must adjust our practice of the history of philosophy, our practice of history and of philosophy, to this reality, which was also a chance and which more than ever remains a chance"[104] for the impossibility of realizing the headings of a philosophy yet to come. Derrida anticipates the postmetaphysical future taking place along the lines of a debt and duty to the tradition of the past, traced out by the limitations of memory and its openness to an expansion of the difference of itself as the *khora* of the Other. It is not only a matter of affirming the existence of philosophy, but of recognizing and acknowledging its natural right to determine the grounds for asking the questions about its sources, its limits (*peras, linea*), and its future, if only to establish the boundaries of debt and duty that would serve to prepare us for a thinking of what comes next from what came before. "Philosophy," Derrida says, "has always insisted upon this: thinking its other. Its other: that which limits it, and from which it derives its essence, its definition, its production."[105] One cannot beat the antimetaphysical drum (*tympan*) too loudly and still expect to hear the echoes of a timelessness reserved for the task of thinking. Indeed, it would be unwise to "philosophize with a hammer," like Friedrich Nietzsche's Zarathustra, and ponder how best to go about the mobilization of a "noisy pedagogy" that would displace the internal sound of seeming truth in the ears of those poised "to transform what one decries"[106] in metaphysics. As Derrida has warned, "in taking this risk, one risks nothing at all,"[107] for what is *unthought* and therefore *untaught* always already opens the future of a history of thinking and directions of teaching that are "yet to come" (*à-venir, Zu-kunft*).

If an institution—and this word *takes in* philosophy, *imbibes* and *performs* it—is true to its constitution and its name, it must allow for the opportunity to inaugurate something "new" out of its ground (the undying memory of "the old"), to repeat the ethico-political performance of its founding contract and its obligations to the legitimacy of the Other in an affirmative way, "to criticize, to transform, to open the institution to its own future."[108] Derrida explains,

> The paradox in the instituting moment of an institution is that, at the same time that it starts something new, it also continues something, is true to the memory of the past, to a heritage, to something we receive from the past, from our predecessors, from the culture. If an institution is to be an institution, it must to some extent break with the past, keep the memory of the past while inaugurating something absolutely new. . . . So the paradox is that the instituting moment in an institution is violent in a way, violent because it has no guarantee. Although it follows the premises of the past, it starts something absolutely new, and this newness, this novelty, is a risk, is something that

has to be risky, and it is violent because it is guaranteed by no previous rules. So, at the same time, you have to follow the rule and to invent a new rule, a new norm, a new criterion, a new law. That's why the moment of institution is so dangerous at the same time. One should not have an absolute guarantee, an absolute norm; we have to invent the rules.[109]

Deconstruction welcomes the risk of participating fully in the awkward tensions between the conservation and violence of this moment of institution and the originality or newness that it produces. It embraces the opportunity to go where it cannot go and to usher in the impossibility of experiencing an other heading by pushing the limits of the predictability of the possible.

That is what deconstruction is made of: not the mixture but the tension between memory, fidelity, the preservation of something that has been given to us, and, at the same time, heterogeneity, something new, and a break. The condition of this performative success, which is never guaranteed, is the alliance of these to newness.[110]

This may help to explain the reason why Derrida has been empirically and philosophically present—in the role of instigator or invited guest, or both—at the founding of so many programs and institutions. Deconstruction enacts, in itself and for itself, *in the name of being responsible and just, to the alterity of the Other,* an affirmation of the difference of the wholly other (*tout autre*), by mobilizing and navigating the tensions between (1) what is undeconstructible, unforeseeable, *à venir,* to come, and (2) what is deconstructible, the rule of law, its structural security and the foundation itself, so as to create the conditions for initiating something new. And this leads us back to the question of space and place, of disciplinarity and democracy, and the problem of determining *who has the right to philosophy.* Not an easy task, as we will see.

So, is the question of "the right to philosophy" also a question of democracy and of the right of all to participate in the curricular orientation of a public education—for example, who should study philosophy, how should it be taught, what should be taught, and why? And what does this imply for academic responsibility, for the future of philosophy, and for the educational institution, *for the academic responsibility of the institution of philosophy education?*

The question of the right to philosophy is *precisely a question of democracy* and of the validity of its systems of governance, of which the institution of pedagogy is a vital element. For, we well know (and I have discussed this earlier), that public education initially began as a way to educate the subject into citizenship by legislating the ways of the State and its interpretative judicature into the experience of schooling. Leaving the unlettered innocence of childhood behind has historically meant becoming a "responsible member of society," defined via a liberal-utilitarian concept of functional literacy as the ability one has to read and thus adhere to the letter of the law. To be more specific, the idea of willfully exercising the right one possesses to teach and learn philosophy, in moving from the study of law to that of philosophy (*du droit à la philosophie*), constitutes the initial step toward realizing the historico-conceptual groundwork for the immanent reality of the institution of education in a "democracy to come." What would it look like? What would it imply for the right to philosophy, for pedagogy, for the university?

Its instauration would be empowering. That is, its ethic of practice would take into account the right to philosophy from a cosmopolitical point of view by addressing "the competition among several philosophical models, styles, and traditions that are linked to national or linguistic histories, even if they can never be reduced to effects of a nation or a language."[111] Here, Derrida gives a specific example of the directions of a possible heading that can be explored further:

> To take the most canonical example, which is far from being the only one and which itself includes numerous sub-varieties, the opposition between the so-called continental tradition of philosophy and the so-called analytic or Anglo-Saxon philosophy is not reducible to national limits or linguistic givens. This is not only an immense problem and an enigma for European or Anglo-American philosophers who have been trained in these traditions. A certain history, notably but not only a colonial history, constituted these two models as hegemonic references in the entire world. The right to philosophy re-

quires not only an appropriation of these two competing models and of almost every model by all men and women (*par tous et par toutes*). . . , the right of all men and women (*de tous et de toutes*) to philosophy also requires the reflection, the displacement, and the deconstruction of these hegemonies, the access to places and to philosophical events that are exhausted neither in these two dominant traditions nor in these languages. These stakes are already intra-European.[112]

Exercising the right to philosophy from the cosmopolitical point of view would not be the result of any politicized determination of a revolutionary movement or populist gathering intended to reclaim control of subjective agency, of the freedom over thought and thinking, from the *modus organum* of the intellectual apparatus of "the State"—the educational system, including the model of the university—in order to render it unto a nameless, faceless, sexless, and ultimately indistinguishable mass of humanity. This is no route to a contemporary rethinking of the "concepts of state, of sovereignty"[113] in relation to the struggles of actualizing the differences of a new global community as we are experiencing them today. For the efforts undertaken to install the hegemony of an empirico-philosophical ground for "rationalizing" a new structurality of governance, no matter how "egalitarian" or "democratic" in principle, would be haunted by the living ghosts of resentful memories that would no doubt shape the future of a "democracy to come" in a highly reactionary way, limiting its conditional possibility to a negative determination of the moment of institution.

The simple (thoughtless) act of reinstitution unwittingly repeats the appropriatary logic of the hierarchy and reenacts a litany of exclusionary injunctions, both consciously and unconsciously, whether it wants to or not, across the cultural and academic border wars of the right to philosophy from the cosmopolitical point of view. It would make absolutely no sense to attempt to level an institution such as the university, to want to (if indeed one ever could) bring its efficacy to a standstill and make its existence superfluous or anachronistic—even though, on the surface at least, the material formation of its regulative idea and operative ideal may seem quite closed unto the reality of itself, and devoid of any space through which to achieve a productive opening to alterity. Deconstruction is not Destruction (*Abbau*), however. A resistance to the conditions and effects of institutionality must maintain and occupy the discursive form of an intractable questioning that always already takes place from within the language practices of the institution but at its utmost periphery, as Derrida maintains, with respect to the discipline of philosophy:

> Even before one speaks of visible or overriding structures (primary and secondary education, the university, authority, legitimacy), there is the very experience of discourse and language: the interest of philosophy already finds itself involved there in institutions. Everywhere and always, institutions articulate teaching and research, they attempt to dictate our rhetoric, the procedures of demonstration, our manner of speaking, writing and addressing the other. Those who think they stand outside institutions are sometimes those who interiorize its norms and programs in the most docile manner. Whether it is done in a critical or deconstructive way, the questioning of philosophy's relation to itself is a trial of the institution, of its paradoxes as well, for I try to show nonetheless what is unique and finally untenable in the philosophical institution: it is there that this institution [of the university and/as philosophy] must be a counter-institution, one which may go so far as to break, in an asymmetrical fashion, all contracts and cast suspicion on the very concept of institution.[114]

The question *of the right to philosophy* (*du droit à la philosophie*) and of *the right philosophy* is one that must interrogate the "how" and the "why" of justifying the assignation of privilege over a domain of knowledge and its institution within the university to a governing body that is thereby given power to instruct and dictate a judgment claiming, more or less, the force of law regarding the future destination of a discipline and who may or may not have access to it. The intermingling of language with power to augment or repress voice is nothing new. It has always existed, reinforcing the act of institution by fusing the constative and performative functions of speech, legitimizing the seriousness of the scene of founding and all that it signifies as the reproduction of the reconstitution of a body of knowledge into a material form of *praxis*. The illusion of newness enters the world in this familiar way via the difference of the repetition of what is old. And here "the appropriation but also the surpassing of languages" brings back the element of cultural memory in philosophy as that which foresees, on the one hand, "the phenomena of dogmatism and authority" established by the linking of the past to the construction of a universal public knowledge and, on the other, "paths that are not simply anamnesic, in languages that are without filiational relation to these roots."[115] The right of institution accentuates the imperative to control the lines of communication, to make reasons make sense without recourse to the contrariety and complementarity of the arguments of an "other side." The "trick" to a deconstructive defiance of this etiologizing effect, however, is to insert oneself within the openings of the system, at the periphery, its margins, where its center breaks down, where it fissures and cracks, welcomes heterogeneity and difference. "With a sole language [the global extension of English as an international language is the example Derrida uses], it is always a philosophy, an axiomatic of philosophical discourse and communication, that imposes itself without any possible discussion."[116] By not preserving, at the very least, the "due process" of an open and public discussion on matters "educational," and for our purposes "philosophical" also, then justice is not served, is not accounted for, and is thus *not seen as being served* with respect to reinforcing the socio-historical preconditions of an affirmative reconciliation of the Self with the Other in the arena of civic discourse— something that is a necessary and integral feature of the legal and ethical out-workings of a participatory democracy. To be more precise: when one individual or group *has, is given,* or *takes* all but total control of the constructible field of public knowledge (e.g., the institution of pedagogy) and has discreet power over the conditions of its material/cultural dissemination (e.g., a curriculum defines and models its method of teaching and learning, establishes evaluative criteria), then this self-limiting structure of closed governance reinforces the divisive criteria of inclusion and exclusion that make any decisions regarding public education void of responsibility and respectful response to the alterity of another. Such is the power of right, and the sense of its law, for it is forcefully bestowed and exercised freely and autonomously without the necessity of providing a reason, justification, or explanation.

Deconstruction counters the hegemony of a universal language and the monodimensional references of its teaching and learning by stressing the ties between philosophy and the idiomatic. The right to free thinking and its expression without fear of punishment or reprisal characterizes the democratic imperative. For Derrida, this not-so-obvious relationship between the everyday utility of philosophy and what it enables one to achieve in the unique contexts of an infinitely perfectible life-world is what concretizes the value of knowledge and liberates the utterance and circulation of ideas in the public sphere. It is a matter, then, of difference and of democracy, of "putting [philosophy] into operation each time in an original way and in a nonfinite multiplicity of idioms, producing philosophical events that are neither particularistic and untranslatable nor transparently abstract and univocal in the element of an abstract universality."[117] A sovereign monolingualism, Derrida contends, obliges the responsibility of a response by way of a questioning of the question, the legitimacy of its space and place:

> suppos[ing] that between the question and the place, between the question of the question and the question of the place, there is a sort of implicit contract, a supposed affinity, as if a question should always be first authorized by a place, legitimated in advance by a determined space that makes it both rightful and meaningful (*à la fois droit et sens*), thus rendering it possible and by the same token necessary, both legitimate and inevitable.[118]

Would we not expect as much of "imposing and legitimating appellations"?[119] Well, yes and no. Deconstruction would not have it any other way. Derrida poses the problem of the propriety of the question of the right to philosophy, *where and how it should be asked and by whom*, because he knows we cannot refuse an affirmative response to the implications of the scenario; for example, UNESCO is "the privileged place"[120] for inquiring into the right of philosophy. It is a matter of reaching a "proper destination" by navigating the journey of the mission the institution "has assigned to itself."[121] Could we refuse the possibility of arriving at a cosmopolitical utopia? Could we do such a thing, reasonably support its resistance, and still be responsible to the democratic rights and principles that sanction the appearance of an institution such as UNESCO in the first place? The deconstructive "stunt" of offering the reader a choice of impossible alternatives is one Derrida often indulges in. This one is highly rhetorical and dramatic, but not overdetermined in its effects. It defies us to simultaneously agree and disagree, to put our assumptions temporarily under erasure so as to question the premises both of the context of the lecture and of the constitution of UNESCO, whose preamble is laced with the following words and concepts: "peace," "dignity," "democratic principles," "humanity," "justice," "liberty," "sacred duty," "mutual assistance," "perfect knowledge," "mutual understanding," "education," "culture," "war," "differences," "ignorance," "prejudice," "mutual respect," "doctrine," "inequality," "moral solidarity," "communication," and so on. Nowhere is philosophy and the right to philosophy mentioned. The constitution of UNESCO is suspiciously silent in this regard, even though philosophy, in every respect, structures the semantic field of the terms listed above by providing the basis for a conceptual historicity of denotations and associations relating these lexemes to ideas and the types of practices they point to. We still have free will and an open conscience, however. We can disagree at any moment with what Derrida suggests and dismiss UNESCO and its constitution as being "both too naturalist and too teleologically European."[122] This criticism is true enough. And UNESCO does eschew acknowledging its debt and duty to philosophy, preferring as a reactionary and "new" institution to concentrate instead on the securing of educational rights and the profusion of a scientific knowledge that champions forms of research whose intentionality is guided by and directed toward the predetermined ends its constitution spells out. A pedagogy of technological advancement becomes the chosen way to achieving economic success, in turn a precursor to democracy and "cosmopolitical communication."[123] Relating to the effects of this curricular intention, Derrida has an unfulfilled "wish" to sustain and expand an exploration of the extent to which philosophy is "in solidarity with the movement of science, in different modes,"[124] which he expresses in the form of a deconstruct-ive "hypothesis":

> that, while taking into account or taking charge of this progress of the sciences in the spirit of a new era of Enlightenment for the com-ing new millennium (and in this respect I remain Kantian), a politics of the right to philosophy for all men and women (*de tous et de toutes*) might be not only a politics of science and of technology but also a politics of *thought* that would yield neither to positivism nor to scien-tism nor to epistemology, and that would discover again, on the scale of new stakes, in its relation to science but also to religions, and also to law and to ethics, an experience that would be at once provocation or reciprocal respect but also *irreducible autonomy*. In this respect, the problems are always traditional and always new, whether they con-cern ecology, bioethics, artificial insemination, organ transplantation, international law, etc. They thus touch upon the concept of the proper, of property, of the relation to self and to the other within the values of subject and object, of subjectivity, of identity, of the per-son—that is, all the fundamental concepts of the charters that govern international relations and institutions, such as the international law that is, in principle, supposed to regulate them.[125]

Derrida is acutely aware of the fact that "philosophy is everywhere suffering, in Europe and elsewhere, both in its teaching and in its research."[126] This is the motivation for the lecture: to address the rea-son of "a limit that, even though it does not always take the explicit form of prohibition or censure, nonetheless amounts to that, for the simple reason that the means for supporting teaching and research in philosophy are limited."[127] The turn to "end-oriented sciences, and to techno-economic, indeed scientifico-military, imperatives" is culti-vated, sometimes rightly and sometimes wrongly, by the desire for outcomes "labeled useful, profitable, and urgent."[128] As Derrida cor-rectly comments, "it is not a matter of indiscriminately contesting all of these imperatives."[129] There is more to it, however, than a cool de-tachment and acceptance of this narrowed distinction between what teaching and research is needed and what is necessary "in the service of economy or even of military strategy."[130] Derrida elaborates:

the more these imperatives impose themselves—and sometimes for the best reasons in the world, and sometimes with a view to developments without which the development of philosophy itself would no longer have any chance in the world—the more also the right to philosophy becomes increasingly urgent, irreducible, as does the call to philosophy in order precisely to think and discern, evaluate and criticize, philosophies. For they, too, are philosophies, that, in the name of a techno-economico-military positivism—by looking toward a "pragmatism" or a "realism"—and according to diverse modalities, tend to reduce the field and the chances of an open and unlimited philosophy, both in its teaching and in its research, as well as in the effectiveness of its international exchanges.[131]

So, why shouldn't we reject the example of UNESCO and choose to re-examine the nature of its propriety to ask the question of the right to philosophy? As we enter the uncertainty of a new millennium, what does UNESCO have to offer the future of thinking beyond the economic potential and promise of a scientific and technological cosmopolitanism?

To say that UNESCO is not a legitimate institution, a "good" institution, would be to deny the good it has done or can do, to ignore its potential for an effective improvement of what—among other things—it does do well: it fights for access to education on a global scale. Which is to say, it has the capacity and is "duty bound,"[132] in principle, to protect the right to philosophy from a cosmopolitical point of view, even if its constitution does not explicitly say so. And this responsibility is what foreshadows the possibility of enacting a progressive movement of nations, states, and peoples in a transformational enterprise aimed at negotiating the effectivity of a *democracy to come*. It involves taking the risk of affirming that "the stakes have never been as serious in today's world, and they are new stakes,"[133] ones whose formations call into question the very concepts defining human organizations and relations embodied in the constitution of UNESCO: what we in the West automatically accept as self-evident truths about the universal plan of nature and its cosmopolitical democracy Kant made so much of. The violence of authority is not determinate, however. It is subtle, stratified, and discontinuous in its effects, and therefore it must be approached with a respectful skepti-

cism, like that of deconstruction, which lies "between a certain erasure and a certain reaffirmation of debt—and sometimes a certain
erasure in the name of reaffirmation."[134] That is, if we really want to
make our way toward a philosophical reconciliation of difference and
autonomy in light of the colonialist historicity of the West—for "what
one calls, in Greek, democracy"[135] can neither stand nor do without
the presence of real dissensus in its community. So we must be careful not put philosophy "off limits." On the contrary, we must mobilize
the right to philosophy in a way that would address the violence of
authority in democracy by situating its ethical efficacy and validity in
relation to "what today may constitute the limit or the crisis most
shared by all the societies . . . , be they Western or not,"[136] as to the
internal and international negotiation of their future from a cosmopolitical point of view. Again, Derrida's lecture is not intended to
safeguard the boundaries of a discipline that is always already its
Other. It voices the call "for a new philosophical reflection upon what
democracy and, [he] insist[s], the *democracy to come*, may mean and
be."[137] The violence of authority has power to induce silences, but it
does not totally restrict the interpretative engagement of consciousness. Interestingly enough, it can produce a heightening of thinking,
sharpening its philosophical intensity by expanding rather than reducing the human capacity to "respond responsibly," to question the
absolute right and legitimacy of knowledge, its privilege, in an ethical
way, by opening up the self-validating aspect of the institution to the
voice of what is Other. This is the underlying theme of the lecture. It
details the importance of not abandoning the right to philosophy, its
teaching and learning. For what Derrida maintains will and can happen, and what he hopes for, is a reconfiguring of democracy according to a post-Kantian view of cosmopolitanism. Through a fundamental interrogation of the ground of the reason of UNESCO, its
mission in practice and in principle, deconstruction locates the transformative field of its hermeneutic constellation "among several registers of debt, between a finite debt and an infinite debt"[138] that articulate the space between the place of the question of philosophy, the
question of the place of philosophy, and the question of the question
of philosophy—that would, hence, situate the ethical impetus of the
interpretative domain of the institution within the structural locality

of its right to question the question of the right to philosophy as well as the nature of institution and institutionality in relation to the cosmopolitical. Deconstruction, we must recall, is above all affirmation. Its *"yes, yes," "come, come,"* is a confirmation of its unconditional acceptance of the Other rooted in an infinite responsibility *for* and *to* the Other, whose deferral and difference, whose *différance,* it faithfully protects at all costs, without reservation or doubt. Safeguarding the possibility of the question of the right to philosophy, deconstruction heralds the impossibility of a (re)teaching of the Self to be open to learning from the alterity of the Other. That is, the integrity of deconstruction is tied to its original and originary aim of raising the spirit of human perfectibility through its vigilance toward the ethical terms of what constitutes a just response to difference and otherness, and the infinite responsibility that comes with this unprovoked and selfless affirmation.

LAST WORDS: QUESTIONS AND PRAYERS

To return to the question of the right to philosophy and to renew the framing of its articulation within the question of the question. I am referring also to its institutional place of asking, which may also be a space of meditation. A question is like a prayer: its hope needs to be answered—though not always, for a question that in the form of its expression authorizes and is authorized by the law of its origins is always a "prosthesis of the origin."[139] The clash between the interdiction of a line of inquiry and the heteronomy of its language is an obvious dissonance that pushes at the internal limits of the institution. But what of the legitimacy of the "unauthorized question"? In going counter to the authority of "the right to question" by exercising the freedom of its own right to counter-question the legitimated code of a dutiful response and responsivity—the terms of the "responsible response"—does it not also arise from the same ground that it questions, of which it is an *other* part? I should think so. At least, this is what Derrida alludes to—leaves out, yet allows us to fill in—regarding the question of the future of philosophy and who can and should be able to, indeed who should *have the right to*, respond to it.

The ethical dimension interposes itself here again—it did not really leave us—with respect to what I previously called the problem of the "death of metaphysics," conceived as either closure or end. For the incipit of "the question of philosophy," we must not forget, also involves the task of how to go about negotiating the "question of the right to philosophy," and by extension, "Who should do it?" and "Where, in what space?" And here we arrive back at the beginning, where we first started, in the difference of that space between us, me and you.

NOTES

1. See Derrida, *Aporias*, trans. Thomas Dutoit (Stanford: Stanford University Press, 1993); and *The Gift of Death*, trans. David Wills (Chicago: University of Chicago Press, 1995).

2. Derrida, "Tympan," trans. Alan Bass, in *Margins of Philosophy* (Chicago: University of Chicago Press, 1982), xxiii.

3. Derrida, "Tympan," xxiv.

4. See Derrida, *Aporias*.

5. See Jacques Derrida, *Archive Fever: A Freudian Impression*, trans. Eric Prenowitz (Chicago and London: University of Chicago Press, 1996), 3.

6. See Derrida, *Le droit à la philosophie du point de vue cosmopolitique* (Paris: Éditions UNESCO, 1997). With respect to rendering a translation of Derrida's text, I have consulted Derrida, "Of the Humanities and Philosophical Disciplines: The Right to Philosophy from the Cosmopolitical Point of View (the Example of an International Institution)," trans. Thomas Dutoit, *Surfaces* 4. 310 (1994), 5–21. The lecture may be accessed online at www.pum.umontreal.ca/revues/surfaces/vol4/derridaa.html.

7. See Derrida, *Archive Fever*.

8. Derrida, "Between Brackets I," trans. Peggy Kamuf, in *Points . . . : Interviews, 1974–1994*, ed. Elisabeth Weber (Stanford: Stanford University Press, 1995), 5–29.

9. See Martin Heidegger, "The End of Philosophy and the Task of Thinking," trans. David Farrell Krell, in *Basic Writings*, ed. Krell (San Francisco: HarperCollins, 1977), 373–92.

10. On the relationship between death, memory, mourning, and the archive of metaphysics as the cinders of fire and fever marking an opening to the trace of

the Other, see Derrida, *Archive Fever*, and *Cinders*, trans. Ned Lukacher (Lincoln: University of Nebraska Press, 1987).

11. See Heidegger, "End of Philosophy."

12. Derrida, *Archive Fever*, 29.

13. See Derrida, *Cinders*; *The Post Card: From Socrates to Freud and Beyond*, trans. Alan Bass (Chicago: University of Chicago Press, 1987); and most recently, *Resistances of Psychoanalysis*, trans. Peggy Kamuf, Pascale-Anne Brault, and Michael Naas (Stanford: Stanford University Press, 1998), for discussions of the relationship between the death drive and the pleasure principle, and how deconstruction interacts with psychoanalysis.

14. See Derrida, *Of Spirit: Heidegger and the Question*, trans. Geoffrey Bennington and Rachel Bowlby (Chicago: University of Chicago Press, 1989).

15. See Derrida, *Aporias*, and *The Post Card*.

16. An interesting discussion of this aspect of deconstruction can be found, among other places, in Derrida, *Aporias*; "Violence and Metaphysics: An Essay on the Thought of Emmanuel Levinas," trans. Alan Bass, in *Writing and Difference* (Chicago: University of Chicago Press, 1978); and Derrida's farewell tribute to Levinas, an English version of which was published as "Adieu," *Philosophy Today* 40, no. 3 (1996): 33–340.

17. Regarding the question of the right to philosophy see Jacques Derrida, *Du du droit à la philosophie* (Paris: Galilée, 1990).

18. Derrida, "Violence and Metaphysics," 79.

19. See Derrida, *Aporias*.

20. Derrida, "Violence and Metaphysics," 79.

21. *Raising the Tone of Philosophy: Late Essays from Immanuel Kant, Transformative Critique by Jacques Derrida*, ed. Peter Fenves (Baltimore: Johns Hopkins University Press, 1993), contains a fine overview of the "topicality of tone" in the history of philosophy that is the cause and the precursor to the call for an end to metaphysics since Heidegger.

22. Derrida, *Du droit à la philosophie*, 88. (All translations from this text are my own.)

23. Derrida, *Of Grammatology*, trans. Gayatri Chakravorty Spivak (Baltimore: Johns Hopkins University Press, 1974), 161–62.

24. Derrida, *Le droit à la philosophie du point de vue cosmopolitique*, 9.

25. Derrida, *Le droit à la philosophie du point de vue cosmopolitique*, 9.

26. Derrida, *Le droit à la philosophie du point de vue cosmopolitique*, 9.

27. John D. Caputo, ed., *Deconstruction in a Nutshell: A Conversation with Jacques Derrida* (New York: Fordham University Press, 1997), 55.

28. See Derrida, "Où commence et comment finit un corps enseignant," in *Du droit à la philosophie*, 111–53.

29. Derrida, *Le droit à la philosophie du point de vue cosmopolitique*, 19.

30. Derrida, *Le droit à la philosophie du point de vue cosmopolitique*, 19–20.

31. Derrida, *Le droit à la philosophie du point de vue cosmopolitique*, 18.

32. Derrida, *Le droit à la philosophie du point de vue cosmopolitique*, 13.

33. Derrida, *Le droit à la philosophie du point de vue cosmopolitique*, 12–13.

34. Derrida, *Le droit à la philosophie du point de vue cosmopolitique*, 11.

35. Derrida, *Le droit à la philosophie du point de vue cosmopolitique*, 7.

36. Derrida, *Le droit à la philosophie du point de vue cosmopolitique*, 7–8.

37. Derrida, *Le droit à la philosophie du point de vue cosmopolitique*, 11.

38. Derrida, *Le droit à la philosophie du point de vue cosmopolitique*, 13.

39. Derrida, *Le droit à la philosophie du point de vue cosmopolitique*, 13.

40. Derrida, *Le droit à la philosophie du point de vue cosmopolitique*, 13–14.

41. Derrida, *Le droit à la philosophie du point de vue cosmopolitique*, 12.

42. Derrida, *Le droit à la philosophie du point de vue cosmopolitique*, 9.

43. Derrida, *Le droit à la philosophie du point de vue cosmopolitique*, 11.

44. Derrida, *Le droit à la philosophie du point de vue cosmopolitique*, 10.

45. Cited in Derrida, *Le droit à la philosophie du point de vue cosmopolitique*, 20.

46. The roundtable discussion of Derrida's "Des humanités et de la discipline philosophique"/"Of the Humanities and Philosophical Disciplines," in *Surfaces* 6.108 (1996), 5–40, has been reproduced as the second chapter of this book courtesy of the journal *Surfaces*. All further quotations from this text are comments made by Derrida on that occasion, when the text of the lecture *Le droit à la philosophie du point de vue cosmopolitique,* originally presented at the UNESCO conference, was read again for another audience. The page references are from the transcription to be found online at www.pum.umontreal.ca/revues/surfaces/vol6/derrida.html. The phrase "eternal becoming" is quoted from page 3.

47. Derrida, "Des humanités," 3.

48. Derrida, "Des humanités," 3.

49. Derrida, "Des humanités," 3.

50. Derrida, *Le droit à la philosophie du point de vue cosmopolitique*, 20.

51. Derrida, "Des humanités," 2.

52. Derrida, *Le droit à la philosophie du point de vue cosmopolitique*, 14.

53. Derrida, "Des humanités," 3.

54. Derrida, *Le droit à la philosophie du point de vue cosmopolitique*, 15–16.

55. Derrida, "Des humanités," 3.

56. Derrida, *Le droit à la philosophie du point de vue cosmopolitique*, 21.

57. Derrida, *Le droit à la philosophie du point de vue cosmopolitique*, 22.

58. Derrida, *Le droit à la philosophie du point de vue cosmopolitique*, 21.

59. Derrida, *Le droit à la philosophie du point de vue cosmopolitique*, 21.

60. Derrida, *Le droit à la philosophie du point de vue cosmopolitique*, 26.

61. Immanuel Kant, cited in Derrida, *Le droit à la philosophie du point de vue cosmopolitique*, 29.

62. Derrida, *Le droit à la philosophie du point de vue cosmopolitique*, 41.

63. Derrida, *Le droit à la philosophie du point de vue cosmopolitique*, 28.

64. Derrida, *Le droit à la philosophie du point de vue cosmopolitique*, 29–30.

65. Derrida, *Le droit à la philosophie du point de vue cosmopolitique*, 29.

66. Kant, cited in Derrida, *Le droit à la philosophie du point de vue cosmopolitique*, 29.

67. Derrida, *Le droit à la philosophie du point de vue cosmopolitique*, 26.

68. Derrida, *Le droit à la philosophie du point de vue cosmopolitique*, 23.

69. Derrida, *Le droit à la philosophie du point de vue cosmopolitique*, 26.

70. Kant, cited in Derrida, *Le droit à la philosophie du point de vue cosmopolitique*, 23–24.

71. Derrida, *Le droit à la philosophie du point de vue cosmopolitique*, 26.

72. Derrida, *Le droit à la philosophie du point de vue cosmopolitique*, 28.

73. See the comments of Ernst Behler in the roundtable discussion of "Des humanités," 3.

74. Derrida, *Le droit à la philosophie du point de vue cosmopolitique*, 27–28.

75. Kant, cited in Derrida, *Le droit à la philosophie du point de vue cosmopolitique*, 28.

76. Derrida, *Le droit à la philosophie du point de vue cosmopolitique*, 21.

77. Kant, cited in the roundtable discussion of "Des humanités," 2.

78. Derrida, *Le droit à la philosophie du point de vue cosmopolitique*, 26.

79. Derrida, *Le droit à la philosophie du point de vue cosmopolitique*, 26–27.

80. Derrida, *Le droit à la philosophie du point de vue cosmopolitique*, 23.

81. Derrida, *Le droit à la philosophie du point de vue cosmopolitique*, 28.

82. Derrida, *Le droit à la philosophie du point de vue cosmopolitique*, 17.

83. Derrida, "Violence and Metaphysics," 79.

84. Derrida, "Violence and Metaphysics," 80.

85. Derrida, *Le droit à la philosophie du point de vue cosmopolitique*, 16.

86. Derrida, *Le droit à la philosophie du point de vue cosmopolitique*, 17.

87. Derrida, *Le droit à la philosophie du point de vue cosmopolitique*, 16.

88. Derrida, "Violence and Metaphysics," 80.

89. Derrida, *Le droit à la philosophie du point de vue cosmopolitique*, 30–31.

90. Derrida, "Des humanités," 2.

91. Derrida, "Des humanités," 2.

92. Derrida, "Des humanités," 2.

93. Derrida, "Des humanités," 2.

94. Derrida, "Des humanités," 2.

95. Derrida, *Le droit à la philosophie du point de vue cosmopolitique*, 32.

96. Derrida, "Des humanités," 3.

97. Derrida, "Des humanités," 3.

98. Derrida, *Le droit à la philosophie du point de vue cosmopolitique*, 33.

99. Derrida, *Le droit à la philosophie du point de vue cosmopolitique*, 34.

100. Derrida, *Le droit à la philosophie du point de vue cosmopolitique*, 33.

101. Derrida, *Le droit à la philosophie du point de vue cosmopolitique*, 33.

102. See Derrida, "Où commence et comment finit un corps enseignant."

103. Derrida, *Le droit à la philosophie du point de vue cosmopolitique*, 33.

104. Derrida, *Le droit à la philosophie du point de vue cosmopolitique*, 33.

105. Derrida, "Tympan," x.

106. Derrida, "Tympan, xii.

107. Derrida, "Tympan," xiii.

108. Caputo, *Deconstruction in a Nutshell*, 6.

109. Derrida, cited in Caputo, *Deconstruction in a Nutshell*, 6.

110. Derrida, cited in Caputo, *Deconstruction in a Nutshell*, 6.

111. Derrida, *Le droit à la philosophie du point de vue cosmopolitique*, 4.

112. Derrida, *Le droit à la philosophie du point de vue cosmopolitique*, 35–36.

113. Derrida, "Des humanités," 3.

114. Derrida, "Once Again from the Top: Of the Right to Philosophy," in *Points . . . : Interviews, 1974–1994,* ed. Elisabeth Weber (Stanford: Stanford University Press, 1995), 327–28.

115. Derrida, *Le droit à la philosophie du point de vue cosmopolitique*, 37.

116. Derrida, *Le droit à la philosophie du point de vue cosmopolitique*, 38.

117. Derrida, *Le droit à la philosophie du point de vue cosmopolitique*, 38.

118. Derrida, *Le droit à la philosophie du point de vue cosmopolitique*, 9–10.

119. See Derrida, *Monolingualism of the Other; Or, The Prosthesis of Origin,* trans. Patrick Mensah (Stanford: Stanford University Press, 1998), 39.

120. Derrida, *Le droit à la philosophie du point de vue cosmopolitique*, 11.

121. Derrida, *Le droit à la philosophie du point de vue cosmopolitique*, 12.

122. Derrida, *Le droit à la philosophie du point de vue cosmopolitique*, 46.

123. Derrida, *Le droit à la philosophie du point de vue cosmopolitique*, 39.

124. Derrida, *Le droit à la philosophie du point de vue cosmopolitique*, 39.

125. Derrida, *Le droit à la philosophie du point de vue cosmopolitique*, 39–40.

126. Derrida, *Le droit à la philosophie du point de vue cosmopolitique*, 44.

127. Derrida, *Le droit à la philosophie du point de vue cosmopolitique*, 44.

128. Derrida, *Le droit à la philosophie du point de vue cosmopolitique*, 45.

129. Derrida, *Le droit à la philosophie du point de vue cosmopolitique*, 45.

130. Derrida, *Le droit à la philosophie du point de vue cosmopolitique*, 38–39.

131. Derrida, *Le droit à la philosophie du point de vue cosmopolitique*, 45–46.

132. Derrida, *Le droit à la philosophie du point de vue cosmopolitique,* 42.
133. Derrida, *Le droit à la philosophie du point de vue cosmopolitique,* 42.
134. Derrida, *Le droit à la philosophie du point de vue cosmopolitique,* 50.
135. Derrida, *Le droit à la philosophie du point de vue cosmopolitique,* 41.
136. Derrida, *Le droit à la philosophie du point de vue cosmopolitique,* 43.
137. Derrida, *Le droit à la philosophie du point de vue cosmopolitique,* 42.
138. Derrida, *Le droit à la philosophie du point de vue cosmopolitique,* 50.
139. See Derrida, *Monolingualism of the Other.*

INDEX

alterity. *See* difference

analytic philosophy, 11, 28–32, 36, 43, 49, 55–56

appropriation, philosophy and, 10

being, 41, 60

binary logic, ix; and right to philosophy, x

Cavell, Stanley, 30, 31

colonialism: cosmopolitical point of view and, 11, 18n10; philosophy and, 11, 18n10

community: difference and, 73, 77–78, 82; of philosophers, 81; violence and, 77

constative versus performative, ix. *See also* performative speech acts

continental philosophy, 11, 28, 29, 43

cosmopolitical point of view, 17n4, 25, 26, 44, 59, 97; colonialism and, 11, 18n10; democracy and, 98; difference and, 69; education and, 15–16; Eurocentrism and, 6–7; Kant's vision of, 5; philosophy and, 27, 64–80; right to philosophy and, 5–6, 91; universalism and, 5

death of metaphysics, 58–64, 81; deconstruction and, x; right to philosophy and, x

death of philosophy, x, 58–64, 81

deconstruction: and death of metaphysics, x; and difference, 89, 99; of institutions, x, 67, 74, 89, 92, 93, 98; of logocentrism, 63, 64; and memory, 72; perfectibility of human being and, 99; philosophy and, 51, 64–80; right to philosophy and, 11, 89; and science, 13; stereotypes concerning, x; universalism and, 67, 94

democracy: cosmopolitical point of view and, 98; right to philosophy and, x, 13–14, 90, 98

Descartes, René, 47, 48

difference, 17n4, 61; community and, 73, 77–78, 82; cosmopolitical point of view and, 69; deconstruction and, 89, 99; ethics and, 66; institutions and, 93; philosophy and, 10; UNESCO and, 69; unsociability of human beings and, 76; violence and, 78

duty, philosophy as a, 15–17, 27

ABOUT THE AUTHORS

Jacques Derrida was, until his retirement, Director of Studies at the Ecole des Hautes Etudes en Science Sociales. His most recent texts are *Adieu to Emmanuel Levinas* and *Monolingualism of the Other; or, the Prosthesis of the Origin, Works of Mourning*.

Peter Pericles Trifonas teaches social and cultural studies in education at the Ontario Institute for Studies in Education at the University of Toronto. He has taught at schools and universities in North America and Europe. His most recent books are *The Ethics of Writing: Derrida, Deconstruction, and Pedagogy*; *Umberto Eco and Football*; and *Pedagogies of Difference: Rethinking Education for Social Justice*.